GREAT DISCOVERIES IN SCIENCE

Evolution

by Rachel Keranen

Cavendish
Square
New York

Published in 2017 by Cavendish Square Publishing, LLC
243 5th Avenue, Suite 136, New York, NY 10016

Library of Congress Cataloging-in-Publication Data

Names: Keranen, Rachel, author.
Title: Evolution / Rachel Keranen.
Description: New York : Cavendish Square Publishing, [2017] | Series: Great
discoveries in science | Includes bibliographical references and index.
Identifiers: LCCN 2016003474 (print) | LCCN 2016012367 (ebook) | ISBN
9781502619518 (library bound) | ISBN 9781502619525 (ebook)
Subjects: LCSH: Evolution (Biology)—Juvenile literature. | Evolution
(Biology)—History—Juvenile literature. | Discoveries in
science—Juvenile literature.
Classification: LCC QH367.1 .K47 2017 (print) | LCC QH367.1 (ebook) | DDC
576.8/2--dc23
LC record available at http://lccn.loc.gov/2016003474

Editorial Director: David McNamara
Editor: Caitlyn Paley
Copy Editor: Michele Suchomel-Casey
Art Director: Jeffrey Talbot
Designer: Joseph Macri
Senior Production Manager: Karol Szymczuk
Photo Research: J8 Media

Contents

Uncovering and dating fossils helps scientists put together a time line that shows when features like spines and limbs appeared.

Introduction

> I think, at a child's birth, if a mother could ask a fairy
> godmother to endow it with the most useful gift,
> that gift would be curiosity.
> —*Eleanor Roosevelt*

Humans are a curious species. Our curiosity drives us to ask questions and explore the world and universe around us in search of answers. As a result of that curiosity, our species has amassed an enormous amount of collective knowledge, including how to reach outer space and the inner composition of the earth.

One of the most constant objects of curiosity has been the origins of life. How did we get here? How did life begin? How are all of the diverse species we see related?

These questions occupied the minds of the astronomers, physicists, and naturalists of the Scientific Revolution, a period that started as the Middle Ages ended. As scientists studied the earth, they found evidence of an ancient planet that held the remnants of life from millions of years ago. During voyages across the globe they found new plants and animals unlike anything they had ever seen. In the sky, scientists discovered a great and complex universe ruled by laws of physics.

Simultaneously, technological advancements were underway that aided scientists in their discoveries. Telescopes were invented and refined to allow greater studies of the form and movement of celestial bodies. Microscopes were developed, which allowed scientists to discover the existence of cells and, eventually, the minute particles within them. The scientific method flourished, and scientists became increasingly focused on observation-based, testable methodologies.

As natural scientists encountered both living plants and animals as well as fossils from across the world, it became apparent that the species that existed many years ago looked different than the species we see today. Some looked similar and were clearly related. Other, more ancient fossils were unlike anything seen on earth today.

From these revelations came the theory of evolution, or the study of how species change over time. At first, some scientists denied that species could change. Soon, however, many different theories of evolution appeared in the natural sciences. Some of the first evolutionary theorists were unsuccessful in explaining how evolution works, such as Jean-Baptiste Lamarck, a French naturalist. Others, namely English naturalist Charles Darwin, found phenomenal success. Darwin proposed the first widely accepted, comprehensive theory of evolution based on decades of observation. His most significant text, *On the Origin of Species*, cemented the importance of evolution as a scientific discipline.

In the mid-nineteenth century, Darwin put forth a theory of evolution caused by environmental pressures. These pressures caused individual organisms (both plants and animals) to compete for survival. The individuals that are better adapted to their environment survive and pass on their advantageous traits, and over time, these traits become prevalent in a population and the composition of the population gradually shifts.

Darwin's theory, called natural selection, was bolstered by advances in the field of biology. Gregor Mendel's work on plant genetics is often cited as the first published findings of significance on inheritance. As technology advanced, scientists around the turn of the twentieth century gained a greater understanding of what a cell is composed of, how inheritance works, and how variation in populations works in conjunction with natural selection.

Throughout the twentieth century and continuing to present day, scientists continued to investigate the origins of the earth and the evolution of species over time. Today we have greater understanding of how the earth began and how forces in addition to natural selection cause evolution. We know more about the evolution of our own species, *Homo sapiens*, from ancient **hominin** ancestors.

Understanding evolution has helped medical experts understand how diseases appear in populations, how they change over time, and how to treat them better. Understanding the history of how species change over time has helped ecologists and environmentalists understand the nature of extinction and how a changing environment affects plant and animal life locally and globally.

Evolution focuses on changes that began billions of years ago, but its impact on modern scientific disciplines and daily life is enormous. We must understand how we are changing, how the organisms around us are changing, and how the planet itself is changing. More importantly, we need to understand what effects those changes will have. As we will see, evolution and changes in living organisms are well underway presently. Armed with the knowledge of how the processes have unfolded in the past, we can make better choices as individuals, as societies, and as a species about how to go forward into the future.

Aristotle's influential Great Chain of Being model ranked all species on a fixed scale of increasing complexity.

CHAPTER 1

The Problem of a Changing Universe

As Europe moved out of the Middle Ages, the Scientific Revolution unfolded. Our understanding of the world transformed as scientists became increasingly focused on basing hypotheses and theories on scientific observation and empirical evidence. Through careful study, they observed and attempted to explain many phenomena both on earth and in the greater universe.

As a result, the Scientific Revolution involved many different fields, especially astronomy and physics, and gave birth to new fields like paleontology. As developments arose in one field, such as new understandings about the composition of the universe, they posed questions in another, such as how objects move and what forces act upon objects in motion.

One of the most intriguing questions that arose, which we will see unfold throughout this book, focused on where life came from and how it arrived at the forms it appears in today.

INFLUENTIAL BELIEF SYSTEMS and THEIR VIEWS on the UNIVERSE

Before discussing the Scientific Revolution and the changes it effected, we must first understand the prerevolution worldviews that shaped Western culture. Primarily, these belief systems are rooted in ancient Greek and Christian teachings.

These ancient theories of how the universe was formed and how it operated are significant to the topic of evolution because for thousands of years they shaped scientists' understanding of how life was formed and whether or not it could change. In a perfect, divine universe as imagined by the ancient Greeks and Christian theologians, there was no evolution or lasting changes in species over time.

In the Scientific Revolution, astronomy was one of the first fields to show cracks in the idea of unchanging perfection, creating a fissure that spread through other disciplines, including physics and natural history.

Ancient Greek Philosophy

The ancient Greeks and their philosophies were highly influential on Western culture, including Western science. Two of the most influential philosophers in the Western world were Plato, who is believed to have founded the first institution of higher learning, and Aristotle, his student. Aristotle's beliefs were expanded on by a third prominent Greek, Ptolemy.

Plato was born in 428 or 427 BCE in Athens, Greece, and is one of the most famous writers in Western civilization. Of note when talking about the origins and evolution of life, Plato developed a "theory of forms" that influenced how Western scientists understood the definition of species. In this theory, Plato wrote that everything that existed in the world we inhabit had a corresponding form in an ideal universe, and all of these corresponding forms were perfect and unchanging. Academics capitalize the words for Plato's ideal forms to distinguish them from the less-than-perfect forms in our world.

For example, when we think of beauty in the world we inhabit (such as a beautiful person or a rose), there is a perfect

Beauty in the ideal universe that is flawless and permanent. The beauty in the physical world is merely an imperfect representation of Beauty in the ideal universe. By creating this set of dual universes, Plato was able to argue that the universe is perfect while also accounting for the imperfections and changes apparent in the world we inhabit.

When applied to living organisms, Platonic theory says that species are immutable entities (fixed beings). To be a wolf is to be *Canis lupus* (abbreviated to *C. lupus*), and the essence of *C. lupus* doesn't change, even though an individual wolf does over its lifetime. We can understand the idea of a wolf and identify a wolf when we see one because each wolf is a physical manifestation of a perfect essence of *C. lupus.* Because the perfect universe doesn't change, the species of wolf doesn't change over time.

Plato believed that the universe is a product of divine creation. In his writings he describes a universe that is unchanging, eternal, and perfectly ordered, with planets moving in perfect circular paths. Plato's ideas of perfection, order, and permanence left a lasting impression on his students and centuries of Western scholars in regards to the origin and evolution of life.

Aristotle, born in 384 BCE, was inspired by Plato's philosophies on living beings and the perfect, divine universe. He issued his own work on the classification of animals in *The History of Animals*, where he divided plants into more than five hundred species and associated genera.

Aristotle also proposed a model of the universe. In the Aristotelian model, earth existed statically at the center of many nesting spheres, in which the moon, sun, and other planets revolve around earth. This **geocentric** model of the universe predominated Western thought for many centuries.

Ptolemy, an Egyptian scientist of Greek descent born in 100 CE, expanded Aristotle's ideas. Like Aristotle, Ptolemy proposed a model of the universe with earth at the center of a

Aristotle believed that the fifty-five concentric spheres in his model rotated at different velocities, which helped explain observations of planetary motion.

larger celestial sphere that revolves around earth in a perfect circular motion. He also tackled a major problem that faced any astronomer who tried to calculate perfectly circular orbits: With actual observation of the skies, celestial bodies don't appear to move this way.

Ptolemy suggested that the sun, moon, and planets move in small circles called epicycles, and epicycles move around earth in a larger circle called the deferent. Earth is not perfectly in the center of the deferent, but slightly off center. He used a point he called the equant to find a constant angular rate of the deferent's path. According to his model, the sun, moon, and planets travel in the opposite direction of the celestial sphere. Put together, these different circular motions accounted for the observed irregularities of their motion.

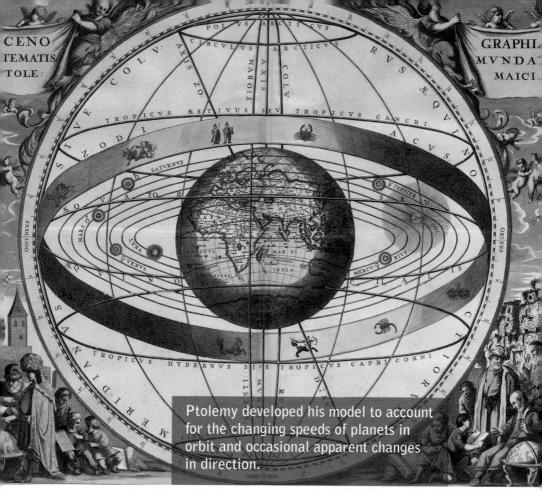

Ptolemy developed his model to account for the changing speeds of planets in orbit and occasional apparent changes in direction.

Ptolemy's model of the universe had great influence on medieval European thought because, though incorrect, his system worked adequately well for calculating planetary orbits. It would take another fifteen hundred years to come up with a new model that replaced Ptolemy's geocentric model of the universe. As a result, it remained plausible to believe that earth was the center of a divinely created, unchanging universe.

Creationism

Christianity has had a significant impact on how people have viewed the origins of life on earth. One biblical literalist, Archbishop James Ussher, estimated in the 1650s that the earth was created in 4004 BCE. His calculation was based on the chronology of Hebrew patriarchs depicted in the Bible. Ussher's work was an immense scholarly undertaking, and though it was not scientific in methodology, many scientists tried to fit their understanding of the earth's history into this time line. Christian views on the earth and its place in the universe, as well as the beliefs of the ancient Greeks, had a strong impact on how Western cultures viewed the origin of life, the history and organization of life on earth, and the earth's place in the universe. Any scientists who suggested that the earth was more than six thousand years old, that it had changed over time, or that the life upon it changed over time opened themselves up to accusations of heresy.

The UNFOLDING of the SCIENTIFIC REVOLUTION

During the Scientific Revolution, which occurred more or less over the fifteenth, sixteenth, and seventeenth centuries in Europe, discoveries in physics and astronomy began to inspire new questions about the earth's age and formation.

While the focus of this book is on the origin and evolution of life, exploring the changing understanding of astronomy, physics, and geology provides context for the questions scientists faced during the Scientific Revolution and how in answering those questions, new questions arose.

The Sixteenth Century: The Copernican Revolution

One of the most notable scientific developments of the sixteenth century was Polish astronomer Nicolaus Copernicus's **heliocentric** theory, published in 1543. At the time, astronomy was a part of a larger category of "science of the stars," which aimed to map the arrangement and movement of the heavens

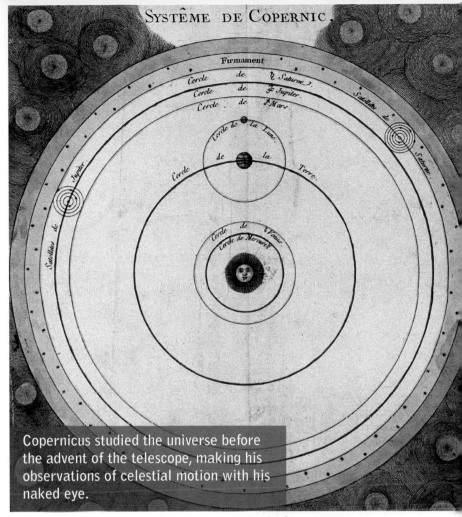

Firmament

Cercle de ♄ Saturne.

Cercle de ♃ Jupiter.

Cercle de ♂ Mars.

Cercle de la Lune.

de la

Cercle

Terre.

Jupiter

Satellites de

Cercle de ♀ Venus.

Cercle de Mercure ☿

Satellites de

Saturne

Copernicus studied the universe before the advent of the telescope, making his observations of celestial motion with his naked eye.

to create horoscopes. The prevailing theory of celestial movement was still that of perfect circular orbits as posited by Aristotle and Ptolemy.

Copernicus asserted that the sun is at the center of the solar system and that the earth and other planets move around it. He provided a method for calculating the relative distances of planets from the sun and placing them in sequential order. Copernicus was also notable for insisting that astronomy must address the real, physical, observable world, a view of science that would grow and prevail over the following centuries.

The idea of a moving earth challenged the idea of a perfect heaven, and the church had deemed such an idea heretical. Nonetheless, Copernicus's books and data tables had such value to other astronomers that they prevailed in scientific disciplines.

Copernicus's contributions to science became known as the **Copernican Revolution** because they fundamentally changed the way the world understood the arrangement of the universe. His work created many new questions in astronomy and physics, as well as other disciplines, and reduced the earth's primary status in the cosmos.

On an earthlier scale, sixteenth-century travelers from Europe began to find and import new plants and animals from across the world. European explorers crossed the globe from India and China to North America, mapping new routes and exploring new territories.

Through these travels, Europeans learned about new species unlike anything they had seen before. They also confronted species that looked eerily like themselves—apes. The new discoveries fostered an interest in natural history and classifying living forms.

The Seventeenth Century: From Telescopes to Microscopes

In the early seventeenth century German mathematician and astronomer Johannes Kepler continued Copernicus's work in astronomy as he searched for mathematical order that could describe planetary motion. He ended up creating three laws of planetary motion, the most notable stating that the planets move in elliptical orbits with the sun toward one end of the ellipsis.

Italian scientist Galileo Galilei also made a significant seventeenth-century contribution to astronomy. Galileo used a telescope, a new invention, to observe that the moon was not perfect but jagged and mountainous. The earth, he said, is illuminated by light from the sun, which reflects onto the moon's surface. Further observations showed that Jupiter had

Scientific Advancements from the Islamic World

Between the eighth and fourteenth centuries, many of the major scientific advancements came from the Islamic world, including significant developments in trigonometry and geometry. One of the most influential Muslim scientists was Abu Ali Hasan Ibn Al-Haitham (known in the West as Alhazen).

Ibn al-Haitham was a physicist born in Basrah (in present-day Iraq) who later moved to Egypt and then Spain. Ibn al-Haitham experimented and published books on the nature of light, color, and optics, as well as geometry, the height of the atmosphere, and much more. He was the first to scientifically explain vision and different parts of the eye. In contrast to Ptolemy and Euclid's theories, Ibn al-Haitham accurately proposed that vision occurs because eyes receive light reflected by objects instead of sending out rays to the object.

Ibn al-Haitham was also the first known scientist to use a camera obscura, and he studied the magnifying power of lenses. Ibn al-Haitham wrote more than two hundred books, but only a few remain, including his *Book of Optics* (*Kitab-al-Manazir*). Due to the impact of his work, Ibn al-Haitham has been called the father of modern optics.

Optics would play a significant role in the development of evolutionary theory as scientists used microscopes to dig into continually more minute particles of living organisms to understand the nature of inheritance.

its own satellites and that the planets orbit the sun, which provided additional observation-based evidence against the old geocentric model of the universe.

These new models of the universe created many challenges to the old orders of thinking. Notably, if planetary orbits were not perfect circles, then new physics must arise to explain their motion through the sky.

Sir Isaac Newton's *Mathematical Principles of Natural Philosophy* in 1687 helped find answers to the questions Kepler's work raised. His laws of motion unified both celestial and earthly physics into one set of laws. Newton also suggested the existence of gravity, which in conjunction with his laws of motion, could be used to calculate Kepler's laws of planetary motion. Many of Newton's other predictions, such as the theory that earth should bulge in the middle, were later proven true with observational data, lending credence to his laws of physics.

Significantly (especially when considering the topic of life's origins), Newton's theory of gravity inspired new models of the earth's formation. Geology, the science of the earth and how it changes, emerged as a significant discipline in the seventeenth century. Scientists questioned the age and origins of the earth by observing the rocks of the earth itself. The layers of rock and the fossils discovered throughout those layers suggested that the earth was made of layers of rocks formed from sediment deposits at the bottom of lakes or oceans over long periods of time. If this was true, scientists observed, the earth's surface had changed significantly over time, and areas that were now dry land must have at one time been submerged in water.

The seventeenth century also saw the birth of two advancements that would become very useful in biology: the discovery of the cell and advanced microscopy. Robert Hooke built a microscope through which he observed cork cells. Hooke's peer, Anton van Leeuwenhoek, famously developed a microscope that had a magnifying power of more than two hundred times, which allowed for many new discoveries of microscopic matter, including bacteria, sperm cells, blood cells, and more.

The Eighteenth Century: Advancements in Natural Sciences

Just as astronomers sought to find order in the greater universe, there were also scientists who focused on finding order on earth itself. In the eighteenth century, scientists made many advancements in natural sciences, or the study of the physical world. In 1735, a Swedish botanist named Carl Linnaeus published the *Systema Naturae,* a classification system for living things.

His classification system divided the animal kingdom into classes: Quadrupedia (quadrupeds), Aves (birds), Amphibia (reptiles and amphibians), Pisces (fish), Insecta (insects), and Vermes (worms and mollusks). Each class was divided into genera, and each genera was divided into species. His system was the first to define genera as groups of species with similar characteristics.

Linnaeus also created a simple naming process in which each species has a binomial (two-part) name indicating both its genus (the singular form of "genera") and its unique species. For example, tigers are classified as *Panthera tigris,* which indicates that they belong to the genus *Panthera* and the species *tigris*. Lions, on the other hand, are classified as *Panthera leo.* Lions are related and visibly similar to tigers and therefore belong to the same genus. They are distinctly not the same as tigers, however, and belongs to the species *leo*.

Prior to Linnaeus, naming practices varied and many organisms had various, often complex names. His **taxonomy** made names more consistent across scientists and became the standard convention. It was a significant contribution to

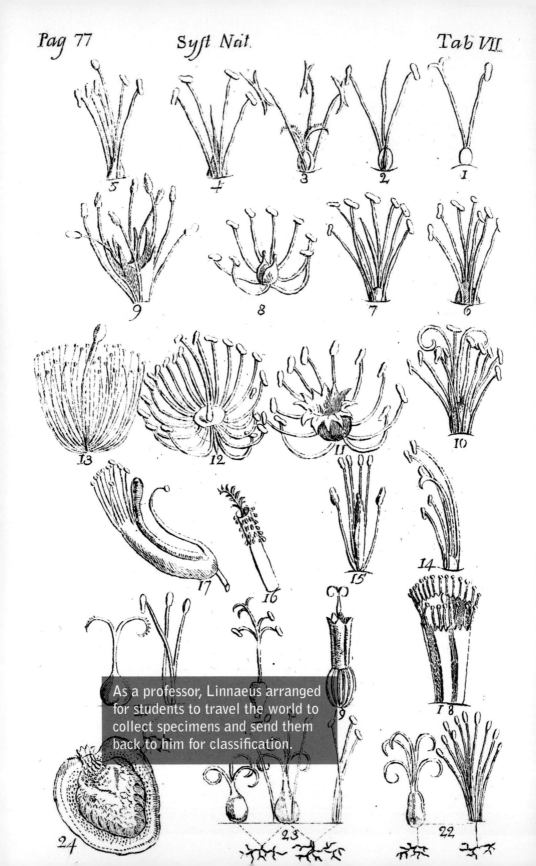

As a professor, Linnaeus arranged for students to travel the world to collect specimens and send them back to him for classification.

science in an era with so much exploration and discovery, and it's still the standard for scientific nomenclature today.

For scientists of this era, natural science was heavily focused on classifying and describing the different types of organisms and less about how species change. They saw differences between species, but not within species over time, a critical component of our modern understanding of evolution and the history of life on earth.

Part of that modern understanding of how species change over time rests in the understanding of time itself. We read earlier that Ussher and other theologians had posited an earth that was only roughly six thousand years old. This relatively brief time period didn't allow for any changes in species on the earth other than dramatic, sudden changes. There was no evidence of such changes on a global scale over the past few millennia, but there was evidence of changes over a longer period of time.

Scientists began to question how the earth had formed and how long ago that process had happened, and many opposing theories circulated during the eighteenth century.

In the late eighteenth century, James Hutton founded a school of thought called **uniformitarianism** in which he argued that over a long period of time, geological processes such as erosion had gradually and continually changed the earth. Hutton pointed to the uplift of the mountains and erosion as evidence of the long, slow nature of geological changes. To make this theory possible, the earth must be greater than six thousand years old (the earth's age according to Ussher's 4004 BCE creation date).

Hutton and those who furthered uniformitarianism had to defend their hypotheses against catastrophists, scientists who believed that the earth had been shaped by repeated, catastrophic events that destroyed existing life and made way for new post-catastrophe organisms. A leading proponent of **catastrophism** was Georges Cuvier, a French naturalist and a leader in the study and reconstruction of fossil forms. Cuvier noticed gaps in the fossil record where life seemingly ceased to exist for periods of time, and he attributed these gaps to periodic floods that caused mass extinctions.

Though the catastrophists did not prevail in the long run, their belief in an abruptly punctuated progression of living forms toward more complex forms did lay a brick in the foundation that eventually supported evolutionary theory.

The Nineteenth Century: Science, Industry, and Progress

The nineteenth century held huge changes for the Western world. The Scientific Revolution continued to unfold and present new theories and discoveries in geology, biology, and more.

British geologist Charles Lyell continued Hutton's uniformitarianism in the nineteenth century. In 1830, Lyell published a seminal text in geology called *Principles of Geology*. According to Lyell, the oceans and lakes are receptacles of sediment and stone as dry land slowly erodes. The location of sedimentary deposition changes over time as lakes fill and rivers change course. These processes can stop and start, creating distinct changes in layers of sediment in a specific area.

Like Hutton, the founder of uniformitarianism, Lyell believed that the processes present today were the same processes present at the beginning of time. (This is why the school of thought is called uniformitarianism—its proponents believed that geological processes stayed the same, or uniform, over time.) We now know this to be incorrect, as many of the forces present at the beginning of time do not occur at present day, but the theory was influential in its time.

At the same time as Lyell was publishing his theories on how the earth changes, England was in the throes of incredible change itself. The Industrial Revolution, which started in eighteenth-century England and peaked in the nineteenth century, brought about the steam engine, factories, and a more technologically advanced world.

The invention of new machines brought both new luxuries and new work. In England, the British railway system grew enormously from about 500 miles (805 kilometers) of rail in 1838 to 7,500 miles (12,070 km) of rail in 1852, connecting urban centers to rural areas.

A **proletariat** (working) class formed in English society, and while many workers suffered in the factories, education became more widely available to all. There were new laws around working conditions and sanitation, and the health and longevity of the population grew.

One important result of the advent of mechanized printing presses and increased education, as well as advancements in the rail and mail services in England, was increased access to literature and reading materials. Encyclopedias in the form we know them today emerged, and people's knowledge levels grew, including their awareness of the changes in many scientific disciplines.

The people of this era believed that they were witnessing a period of change like no other before, and they believed that the rapid changes were moving them toward a better world. The Industrial Revolution was a turning point in history, and its impact reverberated throughout the rest of the world.

From SUPERSTITION to EMPIRICAL SCIENCE

As we have seen, over the centuries of the Scientific Revolution European thought moved from beliefs about the universe based on sacred texts and mythologies to beliefs based on observation of the universe itself.

More and more, scientists sought evidence to indisputably prove their assertions. They began to draw on what we now call the scientific method, which was first developed by Abu Ali Hasan Ibn Al-Haitham. Ibn Al-Haitham's approach focused on systematic observations of the physical world in developing scientific theory and was carried on by Roger Bacon, Kepler, and other scientists.

The scientific method emphasizes making observations, asking questions, posing a hypothesis, experimenting, and creating theories. The goal is to create repeatable, testable, and unbiased theories that explain events and phenomena, from big events like planetary motion to tiny phenomena like cellular division.

Scientists accept that any law or theory that is currently considered true may be later proven false by future experimentation or new knowledge. It's simply part of the process of refining our understanding of the universe, a process that never ends.

CHANGES in SCIENCE CREATE NEW QUESTIONS

The idea that the planet, plants, and even people change over time was initially discouraged because it was a threat to established religious paradigms. However, throughout the Scientific Revolution the evidence of these changes accumulated and eventually became undeniable. With a new focus on the scientific method and objective study of the world, scientists observed the changing universe and pursued explanations for how those changes occurred. Each discovery created new questions to explore. Most significantly for this book, the new theories in astronomy, physics, and geology raised new questions about the origins of life on earth.

Literal biblical interpretations of creation were no longer accepted in the scientific community as explanations for how life began. But if the world was not perfectly ordered and divinely created, then where did life come from? How did it start? In the next chapter, we'll look at advancements in the field of natural sciences and how different scientists attempted to explain the origins of life and changes in species over time.

Scientists use radiocarbon dating to determine the age of a layer of sediment based on how much carbon-14 remains in a sample.

CHAPTER 2

The Science of How Species Change

The Scientific Revolution provided a great deal of scientific material to inspire a closer look at the origin of life on earth. As the nineteenth century arrived, the idea that species could change over time and that life had evolved over a great period of time from a simpler state was an increasingly important topic of discussion.

In this chapter, we'll examine the preliminary ideas and worldviews that made way for a more fully fleshed-out theory of evolution. Before widespread acceptance of evolution, we had to modify our understanding of the earth's formation, history, and age, as well as our understanding of species' ability to change over time. Scientists had to change what it even means to be a species.

An ANCIENT, CHANGING EARTH

The idea of ancient, evolving species starts with the changing understanding of the earth's age and the nature of the fossils discovered in the layers of the earth. How old, exactly, was the earth? Was it possible that slow, gradual changes could have shaped the planet and life into the forms we see today? For such a process to be possible, the earth itself must be ancient.

Scientists Continue to Revise the Age of the Earth

The Scientific Revolution's inquiry into the formation and age of our planet gradually pushed the age of the earth further and further back. In the eighteenth century the naturalist Comte de Buffon estimated the earth was about seventy thousand years old. Some uniformitarian thinkers, including Hutton and Lyell, thought the earth had no sign of a beginning and was indefinitely old. By the end of the nineteenth century, most prominent geologists agreed that the earth was at least about one hundred million years old.

Today, thanks to advances in radiocarbon and other dating techniques, we know the earth to be much older than one hundred million years old. (Scientists have calculated its age to be about 4.5 billion years.) Even this vast underestimate, however, was significantly more than the six thousand years Ussher had calculated using biblical texts. Working with a greater time scale allowed scientists to theorize about significant changes to the earth and the organisms on it that had occurred before world history was preserved in written form.

Scientists Revise Their Understanding of Fossils

When fossils were first discovered, some scientists did not believe they were the remains of living creatures because the idea that the fossil species had either gone extinct or changed over time conflicted with their religious beliefs. Others believed that the fossils buried in the earth correlated to living organisms somewhere in the world. Even if modern equivalents of fossils couldn't be found in England or continental Europe, they thought, they would find such evidence in the New World.

Yet, as scientists traveled the world, they found that other regions had their own unique fossil record and that the living organisms elsewhere in the world didn't correspond to European fossils. Where then, were the living descendants of the fossils found throughout the world? Most scientists concluded that fossils were indeed the remnants of living organisms and that species had likely gone extinct in the past.

When put together in chronological order, there were many gaps between species in the fossil record. To some, namely catastrophists, this was evidence for sudden and dramatic changes in which one set of organisms was annihilated and another was created. For uniformitarians like Lyell and, later, Darwin, it suggested that there were simply more fossils to find and that if the collection was complete, continuity would be clear to see. (These gaps in the fossil record continued to raise questions about the nature and pace of how species evolve well into the twentieth century.)

Lyell is another good example of a natural scientist who struggled to reconcile the evidence fossils presented for evolution with his own beliefs about creation and permanence. Lyell observed that the differences between fossils suggest that different types of organisms had existed over time. He noted that more recent fossils more closely resembled living species than more ancient fossils did. For example, in the oldest rock layers, the Eocene strata, there are many extinct species unlike those we see on earth today. In the most recent strata, the Post-Tertiary, there is evidence of species like the ones alive now.

One logical hypothesis from this observation is that species have changed over time to become the species we encounter today. Initially, Lyell didn't believe that species could evolve, however. He instead believed that over time some species went extinct, some new species appeared, and any adaptations were due to the work of a creator. (He eventually softened his own views on evolution after several editions of his friend Charles Darwin's work had been published.)

Scientists Classify Animals as (Mostly) Unchanging Species

The plants and animals brought over from the New World had sparked an interest in classifying living organisms into species and genera. As they created classification systems, scientists were forced to consider whether species ever changed and became new species or whether a species was eternally in the same form.

Many seventeenth-century naturalists like English natural scientist John Ray had believed that species were the results of divine creation and could change only slightly from the effects of nature. Ray provided many examples of the complexity of form and specific adaptations to environments as evidence of intelligent design, or the formation of a species at the hands of a creator.

In the eighteenth century, natural scientists worked on classifying existing forms. At the same time, they tried to understand what a changing universe (as debated by geologists) meant for species and organisms.

For example, Linnaeus acknowledged some degree of change as he created his taxonomy when he acknowledged that hybridization could create new plant species. He believed there were limits on how much species could change, however, and that all change was somehow part of a divine plan.

Linnaeus's model grouped animals into multiple levels based on similarities. Another model of species classification present at this time was the Great Chain of Being, which harkens back to Aristotle's philosophies. Aristotle believed that all species could be ranked in a perfect hierarchal chain that extended from the lowest, inanimate objects (such as minerals) and extended to the highest divine entity (God).

More than one thousand years later, even into the beginning of the nineteenth century, some scientists still thought of species as links in a linear chain of being. For example, in the Great Chain of Being a dog was closer to a wolf than it was to a horse.

Christian theologians used Aristotle's Great Chain of Being to depict species ranked by complexity between heaven and hell.

Dogs and horses were closer to one another than they were to a shark. Toward the top of the chain, humans fell between animals and angels. The chain was a continuous spectrum of being (for example, flying fish were set between fish and birds on the chain to show continuity) and there was no change to the chain over time.

The absence of living versions of fossils, however, left gaps in that chain. There was evidence that species not seen in current day had existed, but where were they now?

The Great Chain of Being was dismissed by taxonomists as the discovery of new species made it more difficult to fit all organisms into a continuous, linear sequence. The Great Chain of Being eventually fell from scientific favor, and it was Linnaeus's eighteenth-century work that became the foundation of modern taxonomy.

SCIENTISTS DEBATE the GENERATION of LIFE

For millennia, the reproduction process was a mystery to scientists. In ancient times, Hippocrates (the founder of medical science, born in 460 BCE) formed a theory of pangenesis that influenced scientists well into the nineteenth century. According to pangenesis, particles from each part of the body are present in parents' seminal fluids and those particles fuse to form offspring with traits of both parents.

Aristotle thought every part of a new organism was contained in a father's semen and could shape a new embryo out of the menstrual blood of a woman. Leeuwenhoek, born in 1632, viewed sperm cells through his microscope and theorized that they were embryos that gained nourishment from the female egg.

The impact of Newtonian physics, however, had a strong influence on more progressive eighteenth-century scientists. These scientists sought an explanation for all processes based on matter and physical forces, and they dug deeper into the different elements of the reproductive process. The answers they found played an important role in the formation of theories of evolution a century later.

De Maillet's Germ Theory

French diplomat and natural historian Benoît de Maillet was one of the first scientists to argue against divine creation as told in the Bible. He presented his own theory, which included an explanation for how organisms first appeared and how reproduction worked after that.

De Maillet believed in an ancient earth that was originally covered in water. He suggested that at first, germs (little miniature organisms) could have become organisms in the ocean without a parent organism. Once these organisms formed, they were then able to serve as parents to other germs. This idea, that life could form without a parent, is an important development in scientific thought. Like the "Which came first, the chicken or the egg?" riddle, scientists sought an answer for where the first life came from, and de Maillet's theory was a departure from traditional creationist answers.

De Maillet believed that all of the original species were aquatic and that organisms responded to the changing earth over time, a proto-evolutionary view. He did believe, however, that the range of species was limited by the types of preexisting germs present at the beginning of time. Thus, his theory was more static than the evolutionary theories that emerged in the nineteenth century.

Pierre de Maupertuis and Hereditary Particles

The French biologist, mathematician, and astronomer Pierre de Maupertuis was the first to challenge the idea of preexisting germs.

In 1745, de Maupertuis observed that embryos develop by accumulating characteristics over time, not by increasing the size of a preformed miniature organism. In 1751, he published a theory of heredity in his text *Système de la Nature*. In it, de Maupertuis observed that polydactyly (extra fingers) can be passed from parent to child and suggested that the trait is a result of a mutation either parent possessed in his or her "hereditary particles."

From his observations, de Maupertuis produced the first accurate, scientific record of a dominant hereditary trait in humans. Germ theory suggested that any trait present in the adult was present in the original germ. Given his observations on heredity, de Maupertuis thought it was more likely that traits like polydactyly were the results of combining reproductive material from parents to create an embryo than the result of a misshapen germ.

If organisms didn't take shape based on little miniatures, how did they arrive at the complex structures we see? The answer would fall to future scientists.

Comte de Buffon and Internal Molds

The Comte de Buffon was once the superintendent of the Royal Garden in Paris and was also once considered the top naturalist in France. Buffon believed in spontaneous generation, or the idea that particles could form into at least a simple living organism without parents and a reproduction process.

Buffon theorized that as members of a genus dispersed across the world, they entered new environments and changed form in response to their new conditions and food (another proto-evolutionary thought). These different populations became species, which he believed became fixed in their form and characteristics. He suggested that matter knew to form itself into an embryo through an "internal mold." That internal mold was also the limiting factor on how much a species could change over time. Once a species reached the limits of the mold, it stopped changing.

Limitless Change

The theorists we just examined, both religious and secular, believed in either permanence or limited change in a species. Thus, theirs were not full-fledged theories of evolution; they had limited understandings of how reproduction works and the existence of inheritance.

As the eighteenth century progressed, however, some degree of limitless change entered into the scientific discourse. Denis Diderot is one of the scientists who articulated this view.

Like Buffon, Diderot believed in spontaneous generation. In his interpretation of the process, spontaneous generation meant that there was no fixity of forms. He suggested that animals can generate new, useful body parts that they can then pass on to their offspring. These inherited changes can then become part of the species.

PRE-DARWINIAN EVOLUTIONARY THEORY

In the nineteenth century, scientists began to develop fuller theories of change in species over time. First, Jean-Baptiste Lamarck proposed an incorrect but influential theory of evolution. Next, Robert Chambers published a widely read but anonymous text on evolution. Neither Lamarck nor Chambers proposed an accurate theory of evolution, but they were important players in creating a discourse around evolution.

Lamarck and the Inheritance of Acquired Characteristics

French naturalist Jean-Baptiste Lamarck was born as the youngest of eleven children in a noble but financially modest family. He proposed the first theory that can be deemed truly evolutionary beginning in the early 1800s. Lamarck's theory has echoes of the progressive ideal of the Victorian era, as evidenced by his ideas on how species change over time.

After serving in the military in the south of France, where he became interested in the natural history of the area, Lamarck became first a botanist and later a curator of invertebrates at the Musée National d'Histoire Naturelle in Paris. At the time, studying invertebrates was not a glorious job, but the breadth of specimens available provided Lamarck with an enormous amount of research material. He found that studying invertebrates, in fact, led him to study the very foundations of biology and how the processes of life unfold.

Lamarck believed that in nature there is an inherent tendency for species to change from simple forms to more complex and perfect forms over a great period of time. One of the major forces affecting change, in Lamarck's view, is this natural tendency. The other major influence is the effect of the environment and the inheritance of acquired traits. (Lamarck is not the first person to have believed in the inheritance of acquired traits, nor the last, but he is the name most commonly associated with the theory.) He posited that changes in an environment cause changes in the needs of organisms in that environment and they adapt their behavior to meet those needs. The new habits then have an impact on the organism's **morphology**, or the form and structure of the organism.

According to Lamarck, using a certain body part more or less changes the body part. Using an organ or body part more strengthens, develops, and even enlarges it (which we see evidence of when we lift weights or exercise). Using an organ or body part less weakens it. In Lamarck's theory, this change can

Lamarck invented the name "invertebrates" for animals without a backbone after being appointed to study worms and insects at the Musée National d'Histoire Naturelle.

be passed on through generations to cause a gradual change in the size or shape of body parts based on use and disuse.

For example, Lamarck believed that birds that live in water (like ducks) continually stretch their toes to propel themselves through water better. Over time, the continual stretching causes the development of webbed feet in water birds. Meanwhile, birds that perch in trees stretch and curl their toes until they have longer, curved toes. Birds that live on the periphery of water (such as egrets) continually stretch their legs and necks so they can keep their bodies dry while standing and eating, and they develop long legs and necks as a response.

Lamarck believed that species do not go extinct, they simply evolve into different species. When a species disappears, Lamarck believed, it marks the replacement of less perfect beings with more perfectly adapted versions.

Modern science came to realize that Lamarck's theory of evolution is based on a flawed mechanism (use and disuse) and a misunderstanding of the forces underlying evolutionary change, but that he was right in some aspects of his theory. Most significantly, Lamarck believed in adaptive change in populations over significant time, affected by changes in environment.

Lamarck is famous in evolutionary history as the man who got it wrong, but it is easy to see how he could have thought as he did. The classic example used to illustrate Lamarck's ideas is that of the giraffe and its elongated neck and legs. According to Lamarck's theory, giraffes stretched over and over to reach food, which lengthened their necks and front legs. They then passed this increased length on to their offspring. We can easily observe that the giraffe's body is uniquely adapted for its specific environment and needs, but what Lamarck missed is the mechanism that creates those changes.

Molecular biology later clarified the inaccuracy of Lamarck's theory. We'll delve into the biology of evolution in a later chapter, but for now, it is sufficient to know that **DNA**,

Lamarck believed forms changed due to the constructive power of fluids moving through the body.

our genetic, hereditable material, makes a substance called messenger RNA (mRNA), which makes protein, the building block of organisms. The process does not work in the reverse, and it is therefore impossible for a change in the organism to flow in the opposite direction (from the body to the mRNA to the hereditable DNA). As we'll learn in the next chapter, it is not possible for an organism to develop a change in its lifetime that is passed on through inheritance.

An Anonymous Theory of the Origin of the Universe

In 1844, an anonymous author published *Vestiges of the Natural History of Creation*. It tied together many of the disciplines and theories generated during the Scientific Revolution into a cohesive theory of natural history and the birth of the universe and life on earth. We now know that the book was written by Scottish publisher Robert Chambers, who wanted to avoid any harmful results from the controversy he knew his writing would inspire.

In its opening paragraph, the book shows just how far science had come from the sixteenth century, when Copernicus shattered the geocentric cosmology:

> It is familiar knowledge that the earth which we
> inhabit is a globe of somewhat less than 8000 miles
> in diameter, being one of a series of eleven which
> revolve at different distances around the sun,
> and some of which have satellites in like manner
> revolving around them.

From there, the book took off, putting forth theories of the creation of the planets (from a "universal Fire Mist") to the formation of the earth to the history of mankind (including our evolution from apes).

Chambers refuted the Great Chain of Being classification system, saying, "it does not appear that this gradation passes along one line, on which every form of animal life can be, as it were, strung." Instead, he wrote:

> The whole train of animated beings, from the simplest and oldest up to the highest and most recent, are, then, to be regarded as a series of advances of the principle of development which have depended upon external physical circumstances, to which the resulting animals are appropriate.

In simpler words, what Chambers is saying is that the animal kingdom shows progressive development from simple, ancient beings to more complex beings whose evolution is shaped by and for their environment. Just because we have not seen species change in our own lifetime or even in the last few millennia, he writes, has no significance on whether those changes happened or not. The earth is much older than that.

The book was an enormous success from a sales standpoint. As we read in the previous chapter, advances in printing presses, railways, mail delivery, and education had made for an enormous reading population. The first edition sold out in a matter of days, an indicator of the excitement around the topic of evolution and life's origins in general society.

It's estimated that more than one hundred thousand people read the book in Victorian society (England under the reign of Queen Victoria), including the queen herself. It sold even more copies in America than it did in England.

Chambers's theory had numerous flaws, however. His theory of evolution rested on a hierarchy that species ascended over time, in which a generation of simpler organisms gives birth to a higher type. We now know that evolution is not directed toward constant advancement. He applied hierarchical development to human evolution as well, with adult Caucasian humans as the pinnacle of advancement. This unfortunate theory is racist and without any foundation in science or facts. He didn't have a strong mechanism for how this evolution took place but instead often pointed to the divine wisdom underlying natural processes. However, though Chambers's theory wasn't accurate, it did establish the public's interest in reading and discussing evolutionary theory.

The ECONOMIC FOUNDATION of EVOLUTIONARY THEORY

One of the major components of what would become Darwin's widely accepted theory of evolution came from the realm of economics. Thomas Robert Malthus, an English cleric and scholar, wrote an influential and famous piece titled *An Essay on the Principle of Population*. In it, Malthus wrote:

> Population, when unchecked, increases in a geometrical ratio. Subsistence increases only in an arithmetical ratio. A slight acquaintance with numbers will shew the immensity of the first power in comparison of the second…This implies a strong and constantly operating check on population from the difficulty of subsistence.

Malthus writes that this scarcity of resources (food and habitat) exists in both the human realm as well as the rest of the animal and vegetable kingdoms. Checks, as he calls them, are the factors that limit one side of an equation. In this case, a relative lack of resources is a check on unlimited population growth. When population growth is not checked and resources grow scarce due to high consumption, "the poor consequently must live much worse, and many of them be reduced to severe distress."

Malthus's students called him "Pop Malthus" or "Population Malthus."

In humans, Malthus writes, this creates an oscillation, or a swing back and forth between conditions. During periods of high population growth, the poor are plentiful and so pinched for resources that they put off marriage and reproduction. This then decreases the size of the next generation. Meanwhile, the rich are able to employ the many poor people at a low wage. Increased employment increases agriculture yields and the supply of resources. Supply meets demand again, if momentarily, before the encouraged population once again grows faster than resources.

The Groundwork of Evolutionary Theory Is Laid

Here we arrive at a point where geologists are positing an ever more ancient earth and natural scientists have moved to theories in which species can change over time—and perhaps even originate spontaneously without parental organisms. We have evidence of ancient fossil organisms that no longer exist today and theories of evolution that try to explain how this came to be. Malthus's economics, seemingly unconnected, discuss the constant struggle for existence when populations grow faster than their supply of resources can support. These scientific and scholarly advancements set the scene for the work of Charles Darwin, who proposed the first widely accepted theory of evolution.

The Life of Thomas Robert Malthus

Thomas Robert Malthus was born in February of 1766 in Surrey, England, to a wealthy and well-connected family (his great grandfather Daniel Malthus, an apothecary, personally served Queen Anne and King George I).

He attended Jesus College, Cambridge. He later served as the parson in a country church, where he saw many children who ate bread as their primary food, ran barefoot for lack of shoes, and lived in rudimentary housing. Birth rates in England were high at that time, and it is estimated that about one-quarter of the population was younger than ten, half younger than twenty.

Malthus published his first edition of *An Essay on the Principle of Population* in 1798 and released five subsequent versions to add new material and perspectives and address criticism. In 1805, Malthus became a professor of history and political economy at the East India College in Hertfordshire.

Contrary to the common theme of advancement and progress in the nineteenth century, Malthus didn't believe that society was advancing to a better state. He also disagreed with the English Poor Laws, the welfare system that provided work and aid to the poor. He believed that the total effect was to increase the number of poor people by making poverty more comfortable without increasing the resources available to them, worsening their conditions overall.

Malthus became a prominent figure in debates about population and policy and though criticized, was considered one of the (perhaps the singular) most prominent living political economists of his day.

At Edinburgh, Darwin studied alongside radical students who were barred from Oxford and Cambridge for deviating from Anglican orthodoxy.

CHAPTER 3

The Major Players in the Discovery of Evolution

C harles Darwin published the world's first compelling, groundbreaking work on how evolution works, and he is heralded as the father of evolution. As we saw in the last chapter, Darwin wasn't the first scientist to have posited that species evolve over time, but he was the first to thoroughly change the way scientists view the process of evolution and how it unfolds.

Darwin's theory of evolution wasn't perfectly accurate either (science is always a process of making and revising hypotheses and theories). Just the same, his understanding of the role of the environment and **natural selection** in evolution made his the foundational theory of evolution to this day. Darwin's work was a sensation at the time that he published his theory, and it continues to shape how scientists in the modern era approach evolution.

Darwin's theory was only partially accepted at the time of publication. He proposed a mechanism for how evolution works that needed additional (and deeper) science to be truly understood. Gregor Mendel's work in genetics and inheritance was an influential factor in filling in the missing pieces, both because of the work Mendel did himself and the work that he inspired decades later in scientists like Thomas Hunt Morgan.

The work by Mendel and his successors became an essential component of what is now called Darwinian evolution.

As we'll see in the next chapter, additional scientific discoveries in the twentieth century have continued to shape our understanding of evolution and the mechanisms and forces at play. In this chapter, we'll focus on the scientists, Darwin and Mendel, who laid the groundwork for our initial understanding.

CHARLES DARWIN

Charles Darwin was born in 1809 to a wealthy family. His grandfather, Erasmus Darwin, was a poet, physician, and naturalist. His father, Robert Darwin, was a physician, and his mother, Susannah, was the daughter of the famous potter Josiah Wedgwood, who industrialized the production of pottery. (Wedgwood pottery and china is still well known today.)

As a young child, Charles Darwin was not considered particularly intelligent or promising, but he loved collecting shells, minerals, and other items. He didn't spend much time classifying his collection, he wrote in his autobiography. Instead he simply enjoyed their beauty. He also enjoyed bird watching and other outdoor activities.

Darwin began his advanced education by pursuing a medical degree at the University of Edinburgh, where he studied with Robert Grant, an advocate for Lamarck's theory of evolution. Darwin's initial impressions of Lamarck had been unremarkable, but he was inspired to read Lamarck's work again.

Darwin disliked his medical studies and eventually switched schools to attend Cambridge, where he pursued a religious studies degree. His goal was to become a country parson (minister) so that he might study natural history in relative peace. At the time, he took a strict, literalist interpretation of the Bible, though he questioned the practices of the Church of England.

While at Cambridge, he took botany courses and read William Paley's *Natural Theology* (among his other works). Studying Paley was one of the most valuable takeaways he gained from his formal education. Darwin was at this point still a passionate naturalist, growing his childhood fascinations with nature and collections into a true academic pursuit.

At Cambridge, Darwin made friends with professors that would change the course of his life. He befriended a Professor Henslow who was an expert in botany, mineralogy, geology, and many other sciences. Henslow held weekly science gatherings where Darwin met many other scientists. When another professor organized a geology expedition to North Wales in 1831, Henslow arranged for Darwin to go along. They spent the trip looking for fossils and marking rock stratifications.

Darwin's Great Adventure

When he got home from Wales, Darwin was invited to embark on a journey on the HMS *Beagle* that would ultimately last for five years. Darwin sailed with Captain Robert Fitzroy, who was assigned to survey Patagonia and Tierra del Fuego as well as the shores of Chile and Peru, and to make complete longitudinal measurements around the world. Darwin was to serve as a naturalist and companion for the captain. (Of note: The captain of the HMS *Beagle* later told Darwin he almost forbade Darwin from coming along because the captain believed he could tell a person's character from the outline of his face, and he didn't think Darwin's nose indicated the right character of energy for the voyage. Though the Scientific Revolution was well under way, pseudoscience was still strong!)

Darwin witnessed phenomena both beautiful and terrifying on his voyage, from tropical rain forests to parasitic wasps to war.

SARMIENTO IN THE DISTANCE. *Frontispiece*

The HMS *Beagle* trip was both a fantastic adventure and a life-changing event in Darwin's life. As a naturalist, he spent much of his time studying and describing the geology, plants, and animals he saw each time the ship stopped. Darwin saw the effects of an 1835 earthquake in Chile, including a coastline that had risen by 10 feet (3 meters). He found large fossils that were clearly related to modern South American animals, including llamas, opossums, and armadillos. He observed different species of a South American flightless bird, the rhea, that competed in overlapping territories in Patagonia. He observed isolated oceanic islands in the Galápagos Archipelago and the distinctive varieties of animals that lived on separate islands.

In one case, Darwin found giant tortoises in the Galápagos that weighed hundreds of pounds. The inhabitants of the islands told Darwin they could identify which island a tortoise came from based on how it looked, for each island had a distinctive variety. Darwin was fascinated by this, as the islands

In the Cape Verde Islands, his first stop, Darwin saw seashells on a cliff and hypothesized that the cliff had once been underwater.

were similar in appearance and in plant life, though they were geographically isolated. Similarly, the different Galápagos Islands were home to unique varieties of finches, including a wide array of beak sizes and shapes. At first, Darwin didn't realize they were all finches because they were so different (another scientist pointed it out when Darwin returned home). The implications of his findings shaped the rest of Darwin's career and the future of the natural sciences.

While Darwin sailed on the HMS *Beagle*, he read the first volume of Lyell's *Principles of Geology*, which, as we discussed in the first chapter, proposes that the same gradual forces have been shaping the earth throughout time. Darwin saw evidence of the earth's changing surface on his voyage, from the beds of sedimentary rock in the Cape Verde Islands lifted from the ocean floor by volcanic activity to coral reefs growing on sinking ocean beds. He found Lyell's book incredibly valuable for understanding the geology he saw.

In earlier times, scientists had thought that other parts of the world might contain living examples of Europe's fossils. Darwin found no such evidence. Instead, throughout his journey, Darwin compiled a huge amount of evidence for an earth and living organisms that changed over time.

Darwin returned to England in 1836, after which point he published several books with his observations from the HMS *Beagle* trip, including *The Voyage of the Beagle* in 1845 and *Structure and Distribution of Coral Reefs* in 1842. He spent almost twenty-five years, however, working on his theory of the origin of the species and the interplay of environment and evolution.

In the meantime, when Darwin first returned, he served as a secretary in the Geological Society and presented many pieces of work to the society, including papers on earthquakes and erratic boulders of South America. He visited frequently with Lyell, whom Darwin considered to have contributed the most to geology. Lyell opposed Lamarck's theory of acquired trait inheritance and initially didn't accept Darwin's theory of evolution. Lyell was interested in Darwin's work on coral reefs, however, and they had much to talk about. Lyell was a valuable friend, Darwin wrote, because he forced Darwin to present a case for any hypothesis and challenged him thoroughly.

In 1838, Darwin read Malthus's essay on population "for amusement," and this provided him with the mechanism for evolution that he had been looking for. All animals and plants are in a struggle for existence, he surmised, and those with more favorable variations in their given environments will live while the others will die. From this process, Darwin envisioned, new species would gradually form over time.

In 1842, he wrote his first short abstract of his theory. In this same year, Darwin and his wife, Emma (a Wedgwood cousin), left London for the country, where his health was better and he could focus his time on working and writing. Darwin was relatively reclusive, leaving home only for short visits to family members and trips to the sea. He enjoyed daily walks, spending time in the garden, and riding horses. He responded to the many letters he received from fellow scientists and fans of his work. And, of course, Darwin worked.

In 1844, Darwin expanded his short abstract into a longer version, which he continued to work on for many more years. As he wrote, Darwin kept his ideas private, except for a few very close friends.

Darwin took an extraordinarily long time developing and writing his theory. First, he didn't immediately have answers to the mechanisms for the variation between species he had observed on the HMS *Beagle*. He wanted to think through his theories, once he formed them, for as long as possible before becoming set on a course of thought. Moreover, he wanted to present a thorough examination of evidence so that he could avoid the accusations of heresy that plagued his predecessors, including Chambers after his book *Vestiges*.

His theory, which we'll discuss in greater detail in the next chapter, proposed that species evolve gradually and continually over time in response to changes in their environment and competition for resources. Variation is always present in offspring, and the variations that are most beneficial for survival become increasingly prevalent within communities, causing populations to evolve over time.

In 1858, another scientist, Alfred Russell Wallace, sent Darwin a paper that posited nearly the same theory of evolution that Darwin had derived. Wallace had also traveled internationally, observed the effects of geographic distribution of plants and animals, and read Malthus's theory. The two men had remarkably similar building blocks and arrived at similar theories around the same time. Darwin now had a strong impetus (scholarly competition) to actually publish his work.

Darwin and Wallace presented papers on evolution together at a meeting of the Linnaean Society in London and, at the time, neither paper attracted much attention. A year later, Darwin published his seminal work, *On the Origin of Species,* which was an immediate success. The first print run sold out on the day of its publication, and a second edition sold out soon afterward. By this time, Darwin was a well-known natural scientist and had so much evidence that people respected his ideas, even if they didn't fully believe in them. Additionally, he had anticipated objections and proposed a testable mechanism for evolution that firmly grounded theories of evolution in the scientific method.

Within a decade, Darwin's theory of evolution prevailed in the scientific community. At the same time, most scientists didn't accept natural selection as the mechanism for how that evolution took place.

Some scientists said that the precursors of complex traits (such as the heart or eyes) wouldn't have been advantageous and therefore natural selection couldn't have selected for transitional forms. Another objection—which was later proven false—was that there wasn't enough geological time for Darwin's theory of life's origins to have unfolded. A more significant objection rested on the erroneous idea of **blended inheritance**. In this theory of inheritance, unique variations were thought to be lost through the generations as they blended into an average of parental traits passed on and blended in offspring.

In the 1880s and 1890s, other theories, such as resurgences of Lamarckism, **saltationism** (in which new species are formed by large, nongradual changes), and orthogenesis (in which populations have an inherent tendency to change in some direction), were more popular than natural selection as the mechanisms of evolution.

It wasn't until scientists revisited the work of Gregor Mendel, published in 1866 and brought to a place of

Darwin and the Scientific Method

I had ... followed a golden rule, namely, that whenever a published fact, a new observation, or thought came across me, which was opposed to my general results, to make a memorandum of it without fail and at once ... Owing to this habit, very few objections were raised against my views which I had not at least noticed and attempted to answer.

This quote from Darwin's autobiography highlights one of the reasons why Darwin enjoyed such great scientific and public success. He applied great rigor to finding evidence for his theories, which he laid out in *On the Origin of Species* and other texts.

Darwin spent several decades working on his theory of evolution via natural selection. He first wrote nothing at all, then an abstract, and then a much longer manuscript. Taking a slow approach with few words committed to the page allowed him to challenge his own theories more freely. Not a single one of his hypotheses went unchanged, he wrote, and some were discarded entirely. He strived to select the most compelling facts and arguments, and the numerous case studies he presented in his book helped establish the credibility of his ideas about evolution.

Darwin's approach is a good example of practicing the scientific method. He kept his mind open and challenged his own ideas from many angles in order to be sure they would stand against objections.

significance in the early twentieth century, that they understood the mechanisms beneath the variations and inheritance of traits and natural selection. At the time of writing his book, Darwin knew that traits were inherited, but he admitted he himself did not know how the laws of inheritance work. Of note, Darwin had not read Mendel.

GREGOR MENDEL

The debates that took place in the nineteenth century around natural selection were heavy with ignorance around how inheritance works. Moravian monk and scientist Gregor Mendel had studied genetics and inheritance in the middle of the nineteenth century, and at the time of publication, little importance was attributed to his work.

Mendel was a little-known scientist and published his work in a little-known journal. Additionally, at the time, his theories were not necessarily considered revolutionary, and though many who studied hybridization knew of his paper, it didn't cause a big scientific sensation.

Mendel was born in 1822 in Heinzendorf bei Odrau on the Moravian-Silesian border (today Hynčice, Czech Republic). His mother was the daughter of a gardener, his father had served as a soldier in the Austrian army and later grew fruit trees and kept bees in the family's yard. Mendel was a bright student and was selected by the teachers in his own village to attend a school farther away.

Mendel was able to attend university, where he studied religious studies and sciences, before joining an Augustinian monastery in Brno where he could continue his own studies in addition to completing his monastery duties. When he entered the monastery, he cared for a garden there used to grow rare Moravian plants.

In 1848, Mendel began studies at Vienna University, where he learned physics, research methodologies, probability,

Mendel's plant experiments drew on
his previous coursework in physics
and mathematics, helping him express
inheritance ratios in binomial equations.

The monastery supported Mendel's hybridization experiments in part because the results could impact future profits of the monastery's wool sales.

and plant hybridization, which anticipated his most famous contributions to science.

Mendel's most famous work revolves around his pea plant experiments and the effects of hybridization. Mendel bred and studied peas (among other species of plants) for fifteen years. He examined the effects of crossing varieties of peas on distinct traits like round versus wrinkled seeds and the position of flowers on the plants.

Each "character," he wrote, is determined by a pair of elements, one from each parent. He argued that characters, later understood as **genes**, remain intact from one generation to the next and are not blended. Instead, characters are dominant or recessive, which affects whether or not they appear in offspring.

As mentioned above in the section on Darwin, one of the biggest criticisms of Darwin's evolution theory was that variation would disappear as changes in traits blended into an average over generations. Mendel's emphasis on the distinct nature of traits over generations helps lay this objection to rest.

Like Darwin, Mendel did not have a completely original or completely fleshed-out theory. Yet close rereading of his work on plant genetics helped other scientists develop laws of genetics and inheritance that filled the missing gap around the theory of natural selection and evolution. In 1900, three different European scientists working on plant hybridization (Hugo DeVries, Carl Correns, and Erich von Tschermak) independently rediscovered Mendel's works and brought it back into scientific discourse.

One of the factors that led to the rediscovery of Mendel's work was a surging interest in cytology (the study of the structure of cells) toward the end of the nineteenth century. Scientists had determined that organisms are made of cells and that the nucleus of a cell shaped its form. The field of cytology expanded into greater understandings of sexual reproduction and inheritance, and DeVries, Correns, and Tschermak discovered Mendel's work in pursuit of their own studies of plant genetics.

After the rediscovery, a notable advocate of Mendel's work was William Bateson, a Cambridge zoologist who read Mendel's work in 1900. Bateson disagreed with Darwin's theory of evolution driven by continuous variation, and in 1894 he had published his own theory of evolution driven by discontinuous variation. Bateson used Mendel's work to declare a new field of science, genetics, and had Mendel's work republished in English-language journals and books.

How then, did science once used by anti-Darwinists become the linchpin in Darwinism? The key lies in understanding the nature of genetic variation in populations and its relationship to natural selection.

The MODERN SYNTHESIS

At the beginning of the twentieth century, the field of biology was divided into different camps that disagreed on how evolution works. The main divide was between Mendelian genetics and Darwinian natural selection. Those who focused on Mendelian genetics spent more time in the lab focusing on

Dark peppered moths were unheard of before the Industrial Revolution. After industrialization, they were the dominant form.

the mechanisms for variation, while Darwinians focused on how natural populations adapted to changing circumstances. The two segments had very different approaches and research methodologies.

In the Mendelian camp, scientists such as Thomas Hunt Morgan were making significant discoveries, including Morgan's discovery of the role of **mutations** in increasing variation in populations. Meanwhile, Darwinians were studying the effects of natural selection, including a famous study on *Biston betularia*, the peppered moth. Dark peppered moths had become significantly more prevalent in the English city of Manchester's moth populations after the Industrial Revolution. The moths became a classic example of natural selection in action.

The first steps toward merging Mendelian and Darwinian scientists came with the formation of a new field called population genetics. Three scientists were especially instrumental in establishing the new field: R. A. Fisher, Sewall Wright, and J.B.S. Haldane.

In 1918, Fisher wrote a paper on the effects of Mendelian genetics in conjunction with nongenetic factors on the correlation of traits in relatives. Wright studied the effects of inbreeding on the evolution of populations, such as mutation, which he wrote about in 1921. Haldane studied how Mendelian variation in a population affects survival and reproduction, thus creating a change in the population over time. The three scientists had different ideas of how exactly evolution worked, but all three united both Darwinian concepts of natural selection and Mendelian genetics in their work.

Merging Darwin and Mendel into population genetics made way for a larger synthesis amid biologists called the Modern Synthesis. Numerous scientists helped pave the way for the merger, including Ukrainian scientist Theodosius Dobzhansky, who worked in Morgan's lab. Dobzhansky's contributions included showing that there is enough genetic variation in natural populations for natural selection to work. Another scientist, George Gaylord Simpson, showed that the evolutionary change seen in the fossil record was compatible with population genetics. With an increase in work drawing on both natural selection and population genetics, the fields merged and a new discipline was born: evolutionary biology.

Since then, as is common in science, scientists have continued to make new hypotheses and discoveries around the mechanisms involved in evolution and debate the significance of these findings. We'll learn more about how our understanding of evolution has continued to change in the final chapter of this book.

FOUNDING FATHERS

Darwin's and Mendel's work began centuries of research into natural selection, evolution, and genetics. Both scientists spent long periods of time observing natural processes, noting results, and putting forth theories that could explain what they saw. They were limited by the constraints of the technology available in their day, but from the data they gathered, they wrote foundational theories of evolution and genetic variation and inheritance.

In the next chapter, we'll look deeper into how natural selection, inheritance, and population genetics work.

Scientists have recently discovered genetic variations underlying the differences in finch beak morphology.

CHAPTER 4

The Discovery of Evolution

When Charles Darwin published his most important work, *On the Origin of Species*, in 1859, he put forth a theory of evolution that launched an era of inquiry into how life began and how it changes over time. He wrote in a time before there was a clear understanding of genetics or inheritance, and through careful study and observation of the natural world, he came up with an astounding hypothesis.

Darwin's work was heavily inspired by the new flora, fauna, and fossils he saw on his trip to South America on the HMS *Beagle*. The trip had provoked many questions in Darwin about how such prolific organic diversity had arisen, as well as how living species correlated to the fossils found in the ground. While on board the *Beagle*, he focused on collecting and organizing (sometimes haphazardly) his specimens. After he returned to England, he dedicated his time to finding a theory that could account for the diversity of life and changes over time.

DARWIN'S THEORY: EVOLUTION THROUGH NATURAL SELECTION

Darwin saw that variation is always present in populations of plants and animals. "No one supposes that all the individuals of the same species are cast in the very same mould," he wrote in *On the Origin of Species*. In humans, parents produce children who all look somewhat similar but also different. Children of different parents look even more different from one another, though they're still clearly human. This natural variation extends from humans, where we can easily see its presence in our family members, friends, and strangers, to all other organisms.

When variations begin to accumulate over time, populations change. We can see the effects of accumulating variation every time we look at a dog. All dogs share a common ancestor with wolves. There is much more dramatic variation in dogs, however, than there is in wolves. That's because dog breeders have acted on natural variation to produce new breeds of dogs for many different purposes, such as the relatively recent breeding of hairless terriers.

A hairless terrier first appeared in a litter of puppies in the 1970s. From there, hairless terriers were deliberately bred, partly to serve as pets for people who are allergic to dog hair. This process of dog breeding is an example of artificial selection, a process in which humans intervene with nature to select for certain beneficial traits in plants or animals. Due to artificial selection, there is an enormous amount of variation in dogs, from tiny Chihuahuas to towering Great Danes to curly haired poodles.

In nature, variations can appear and accumulate in a similar manner, though usually over a longer period of time. According to Darwin:

> I look at individual differences ... as being the first step towards such slight varieties as are barely thought worth recording in works on natural history. And I look at varieties which are in any degree more distinct and permanent, as steps leading to strongly marked and more permanent varieties; and at these latter, as leading to sub-species, and to species.

Over time, Darwin proposed, an entire species can change to such a degree that it becomes a new species or an isolated segment of a species can diverge and change independently until it becomes a new species.

This portion of his theory was clear to Darwin based on the observations he made in nature. He was plagued, however, by what force drove the process of natural speciation until he read Malthus's work on the struggle for survival in human populations.

Like humans, living organisms are always under pressure from their environment, and they struggle to survive. First, populations tend to increase at such rates that more individuals are produced than the environment around them can support. The disproportionate amount of resources available compared to the number of individuals that consume those resources results in competition for food. Second, predators kill off individuals from weaker species, especially the eggs, the very young, and otherwise feeble individuals. As a result, populations are under pressure to adapt to their environments by becoming better at obtaining food and surviving threats.

The odds of individual survival are not just mere chance; they are affected by the variations abundant in nature. Sometimes, a variation appears that makes an individual better adapted to the environment than its peers and it is more likely to survive.

To use an example from Darwin, grouse (a type of bird related to chickens) are hunted by other birds such as hawks. Brighter grouse are easy to see, while earth-toned grouse blend in with the earth and are less likely to be spotted from the sky above. The individuals with disadvantageous variations, such as the easy-to-spot feather color, are more likely to die before they ever produce offspring and don't have the chance to pass on their characteristics. The individuals with more advantageous variations, such as natural camouflage via darker feathers, are more likely to survive longer and produce offspring. When they reproduce, they pass on their advantageous variations to their offspring. From this difference in survival rates, over time, the proportion of the population with advantageous variations increases, and the look of the population itself changes.

Similarly, the finches on the Galápagos Islands were all descended from a common ancestor. Once on the islands and in geographic isolation, the populations had accumulated and passed on variations that were advantageous for obtaining different food sources. Some had blunt beaks that were useful for cracking tough seeds, while others had pointier beaks for picking up small seeds that lay on the ground. Each type of beak was advantageous for obtaining a different food source, and birds that depended on these unique food sources accumulated advantageous variations accordingly. Over time, the birds looked so different they were nearly unrecognizable as being different species of finches.

The distinct Galápagos tortoises from different islands had a similar story. Most of the species of tortoise exhibit one of two body types: domed and saddle-backed. The domed tortoises exhibit the more ancestral form of the tortoise and live on the larger, more humid islands where food is relatively abundant and there is less competition for resources. Therefore, their shape has remained more similar to the older form as the selective forces aren't as strong. The saddle-back tortoises live on dryer islands and have less food during droughts, creating a selective force. The shape of their shell makes it possible for them to stretch their head to reach higher vegetation.

Darwin called this theory—that useful variations are preserved through enhanced survival and reproduction and create better-adapted populations while harmful variations disappear—natural selection. Natural selection happens over a great period of time, unlike the faster artificial selection in domesticated plants and animals. Sometimes, it has little effect on a population at all. Sometimes, it has great effect. There is no limit, however, to the degree to which natural selection can

Giant tortoises were once common worldwide. Today, the Galápagos Islands represent the only location with more than one surviving species.

modify species over time.

Darwin wrote that for long periods of time, environmental forces are often in a state of balance and nature remains unchanged. Sometimes, however, the balance shifts and natural selection can cause new species to arise through gradual change in the entire species or through the divergence of a new species. As new, better-adapted species are formed, others disappear and become extinct.

Two primary conditions that are likely to cause species to evolve due to natural section are:

- Different environmental factors present in different regions of a species' habitat, given the habitat range is large enough. Individuals living in one region will face different selective pressures than individuals in a different region, and natural selection will favor different variations.
- Isolation of one territory from another, such as through the separation of islands from a mainland,

which creates natural geographic and interbreeding barriers between species. Again, individuals will face different environmental pressures, and different traits will be advantageous based on those pressures.

We can add other changes in environment that create new environmental pressures and cause differential survival rates, including:

- The warming or cooling of an area, such as the global warming occurring on our planet in present day.
- Pollution or other changes in air quality.
- The introduction of a new competitor to a habitat.
- Asteroid collisions that cause extinction events in entire groups of animals, such as dinosaurs.

For example, the fossil Darwin found in Patagonia that was related to the llama (the *Macrauchenia*) was as large as a camel. Over time, the *Macrauchenia* went extinct, and its modern-day relatives replaced it. The same was true for many other species Darwin found fossils and living forms of in South America, such as gigantic sloth-like fossils. Those animals had lived in an environment that favored large animals and were at one time well adapted. They eventually faced competitive pressures from new competitors that arrived via a land bridge (including, eventually, humans). In these new conditions, natural selection worked on the populations, creating some new forms while others went extinct. The new forms replaced the old, and the face of life on earth changed.

Darwin's Definition of a Species

When discussing evolution, it is useful though complicated to discuss what constitutes a species. It is useful because evolution focuses heavily on change in species. It is complicated because to this day, scientists don't always agree on what defines a species.

Darwin acknowledges this lack of consensus in *On the Origin of Species*. "Certainly no clear line of demarcation has as yet been drawn between species and sub-species," he writes. He provided his own definition with the caveat that it was "arbitrarily given for the sake of convenience." A species, Darwin writes, is a group of individuals that closely resemble one another. A new species can be identified when a group of organisms became a "strongly marked and permanent" variety different from the original population.

The Evolution of Complex Forms

Next, let's look briefly at how Darwin describes the evolution of complex forms. For life to have evolved from single-cell organisms to the complex forms we see today, at some point ancestral organisms went through the development of complex organs, such as from having no eyes to having functioning eyes. How could natural selection account for this?

Some of Darwin's critics argued that the transitional forms of organs couldn't have conferred any advantage and therefore natural selection would not have created new organs. Darwin believed that transitional forms did provide advantages to organisms. In considering this process as it relates to the appearance of the eye in living organisms, Darwin writes:

> How a nerve comes to be sensitive to light, hardly concerns us more than how life itself originated; but I may remark that, as some of the lowest organisms, in which nerves cannot be detected, are capable of perceiving light, it does not seem impossible that certain sensitive elements in their sarcode [protoplasm, gelatinous or semifluid matter] should become aggregated and developed into nerves, endowed with this special sensibility.

In *On the Origin of Species*, Darwin digs deeper into the evolution of the eye as an example of complex organ development. He points to certain starfish as an example of living organisms with a more **vestigial** form of the organ: "Small depressions in the layer of pigment which surrounds the [optic] nerve are filled … with transparent gelatinous matter, projecting with a convex surface, like the cornea in the higher animals." These starfishes can sense light and darkness, but nothing more. To Darwin, this state represents the first (and most significant) step from organisms with no eye toward organisms with a light-sensing, "picture-forming" eye. (Note: We and other beings with eyes did not evolve from the starfish Darwin mentions. Darwin uses the starfish as an example of a living organism that demonstrates a less advanced state of an organ we have.)

Darwin hypothesizes that in those organisms like humans that developed eyes, the process started in a similar state with an optic nerve covered in a gelatinous, light-sensing substance. Variation naturally continued in this feature over millions of years, he writes, and through natural selection this variation led to a complex, finely tuned organ.

We often see a trend toward complexity in examples of evolution, such as in the development of a complex organ like the eye. Because of this pattern, and because of underlying religious beliefs, many previous natural scientists who wrote on evolution theorized that species evolved toward "higher forms," usually placing humans at the peak of the hierarchy.

Darwin, however, argued that while species become more adapted to their environments and can in this sense be considered "higher" than their ancestors, the variations that appear are random and there is no inherent direction in the evolution process. Natural selection leads to species that have superior adaptations to their environments, but in some cases, simplicity is advantageous.

Overall, Darwin had a remarkably accurate theory given that scientists of his era had limited understanding of genetics and inheritance. Less than a decade after Darwin published *On the Origin of Species*, Mendel published his results on trait inheritance in pea plants. Though it took some time, Mendel's work would eventually help fill Darwin's knowledge gaps to make the theory more complete.

MENDELIAN HEREDITY

As we have read, evolution occurs because there is naturally occurring genetic variation in populations and processes, such as natural selection, that act on this variation. (Since Darwin wrote his theory, we have discovered that while natural selection is indeed one force for evolution, there are other mechanisms at play as well.)

Darwin knew that variation occurred in species, and this fact was a crucial part of his theory of evolution. He did not know, however, where that variation came from or how inheritance works. Mendel's experiments in plant breeding helped answer the second question by providing more clarity around how variation is transmitted and preserved through generations.

Mendel's Pea Experiments

Mendel's most famous experiments were based on crossing true-breeding varieties of peas (varieties that always produce identical offspring when self-fertilized) and studying the characteristics of the hybrid offspring. What he found changed the way scientists understood trait inheritance and rebutted the idea of blended inheritance.

As an example, consider the color of the pea seeds, which was one of the primary traits Mendel studied. First, he crossed

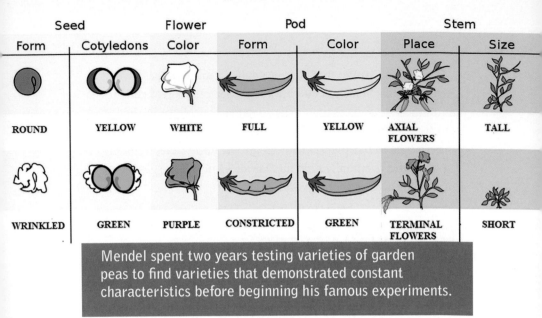

Seed		Flower	Pod		Stem	
Form	Cotyledons	Color	Form	Color	Place	Size
ROUND	YELLOW	WHITE	FULL	YELLOW	AXIAL FLOWERS	TALL
WRINKLED	GREEN	PURPLE	CONSTRICTED	GREEN	TERMINAL FLOWERS	SHORT

Mendel spent two years testing varieties of garden peas to find varieties that demonstrated constant characteristics before beginning his famous experiments.

two true-breeding varieties with distinct colors of pea seeds. One variety always produced plants with green seeds, and one variety always produced plants with yellow seeds. This cross-produced a first generation that Mendel called F1. The F1 generation plants all had yellow seeds.

He then self-fertilized the F1 generation to produce an F2 generation. In the F2 generation, three-quarters of the plants had yellow seeds and one-quarter had green seeds. This showed a 3:1 ratio of yellow seeds to green seeds. The green seeds had reappeared from an all-yellow generation! Variation in seed color continued to appear in subsequent generations of self-fertilization, with some lines always producing yellow seeds, some always producing green seeds, and some always producing a 3:1 ratio of yellow to green.

Mendel studied this phenomenon in many different traits by crossing true-breeding pea plants with trait differences including the round versus wrinkled nature of the pea plant seeds and the color of the flowers on the plants. Each time, only one form appeared in the F1 generation (such as round seeds), and the other form (such as wrinkled seeds) would reappear in the F2 generation. The 3:1 ratio held true in different traits as well.

Mendel's results show a pattern of dominant and recessive forms, called **alleles**. It also illustrates the concept of **homozygous** and **heterozygous**. (Individuals that are homozygous have inherited two of the same allele for a given gene, while individuals that are heterozygous have inherited different alleles for a given gene.) In his experiments, he mixed homozygous yellow and green plants, which have different **genotypes**, or genetic compositions. The homozygous, true-breeding plants he started with can be represented as having genotypes YY (two dominant alleles for yellow) and yy (two recessive alleles for green), respectively. Each parent passes on one form of a trait by contributing one of its own alleles to the genetic makeup of its offspring. In the pea plants, the resulting heterozygous offspring in the F1 generation all had one of each allele in their genotype, Yy. Therefore, they showed the dominant trait (yellow) in their **phenotype** (the observable characteristics of an individual).

In subsequent generations, depending on which alleles the parent plants passed on, the offspring inherited YY, Yy, and yy genotypes and displayed different colors in their phenotypes.

Particulate Inheritance

Mendel's work showed that traits were passed on intact through generations, which is called **particulate inheritance**. One of the strongest critiques of Darwin's theory of natural selection was that variation would be lost through generations because offspring would inherit some blended combination of the parents' traits. Essentially, other scientists had thought that the offspring of a plant with yellow seeds and a plant with green seeds would be a plant with an intermediate shade of yellow-green seeds. Mendel's work showed that this critique of Darwin was inaccurate, and rediscovering his conclusions was a significant step forward for Darwin's legacy and evolutionary science as a whole.

While Mendel had published the results of his pea breeding experience back in 1866, his findings were mostly forgotten for several decades. As interest grew in cellular biology (aided in part by technological advancements in microscopy), a new generation of scientists began conducting breeding experiments akin to the experiments Mendel conducted. As they did, they rediscovered Mendel's work and set out on a course of new scientific discoveries around the basis of trait inheritance.

The BIOLOGY of EVOLUTION

Mendel's work helped answer the question of how variation in traits was preserved through generations of reproduction. Where, however, did the variation come from? Variation appears through two primary mechanisms: mutations and **meiosis**. Mutations account for entirely new variations that appear in a population, as they are changes in the **genome** itself. Meiosis is variation that naturally occurs through sexual reproduction.

Both mutations and meiosis involve DNA processes, which became increasingly more clear after the time of Darwin and Mendel. Friedrich Miescher first isolated DNA in 1869. In 1953, James Watson and Francis Crick (using X-ray diffraction images produced by Rosalind Franklin) determined its molecular structure.

Variation from Mutations

Variations large and small can be generated in a population through mutations, or changes in the genetic material of an organism that can be passed on through reproduction. Let's take a closer look at the genetic material of living organisms to understand more about how mutations and new variations occur.

Base pairs

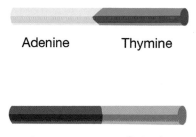

Adenine   Thymine

Guanine   Cytosine

Mutations occur naturally from copy errors and when external influences such as chemicals or radiation exposure break down DNA.

You may have heard people say, "She's got good genes" when admiring a strength in another person. Genes are the units of heredity that pass from parent to offspring and play an important role in determining the characteristics of living organisms. Essentially, genes are segments of DNA found on chromosomes within the nuclei of cells.

These segments of DNA are made of long strings of nucleotide bases called adenine, guanine, cytosine, and thymine. These nucleotide bases are connected to one another within a strand of DNA, and each strand of DNA has a parallel DNA strand that runs alongside it in a double helix. Between these two strands of DNA, adenine (A) always pairs with thymine (T) while guanine (G) always pairs with cytosine (C).

During cell division, the cellular process that creates new cells used to form offspring and continually grow and repair the organism, DNA duplicates itself to create an identical DNA molecule for each cell. This process is called DNA replication.

Another important function of DNA is to make messenger RNA (mRNA), which in turn makes the proteins that make up living organisms. To make mRNA, the strands of DNA separate and one strand becomes a template for producing a strand of messenger RNA with corresponding nucleotide bases. (In mRNA the pairs are slightly different. Instead of A pairing with T, A pairs with U, uracil.)

Each molecule of mRNA then determines the linear arrangement of amino acids in a protein molecule. The order of the amino acids in a protein molecule determines its shape and function. Proteins, in turn, are major building blocks of living organisms and determine the structure, function, and regulation of different body parts.

One easy way to think of this process is "DNA makes RNA makes protein," which is called the central dogma of molecular biology. The central dogma illustrates at a very high level how genetic material flows in an organism.

A News Lens to View Inheritance

The microscope has existed since about 1600, but for centuries scientists were limited in how precise their observations were. One of the limitations came from how light bends (refracts) as it passes through different media such as glass and air. Glass and air bend light at different angles (this is called having different refractive indices), and at greater magnifications, this difference in the bending of light reduces the quality of the image. Poor image quality made it difficult to observe the different components and processes of the cell, which hampered scientific understanding of cellular biology.

In 1878, Ernst Karl Abbe invented the oil immersion lens. In oil immersion microscopy, a scientist places a drop of a specific oil on a slide's cover slip before moving the lens to just touch the specimen. Normally light would refract (bend) in the air between the slide and the glass lens, but in oil immersion microscopy there is no air between the slide and the lens. Because the oil intentionally has the same refractive index as the glass lens, the light does not refract between the oil and the glass and the image is clearer. This improves the resolution of the magnification.

The oil immersion lens, along with advancements in cell fixing methods and dyes, allowed scientists to identify the major cell organelles, including mitochondria, the endoplasmic reticulum, and the golgi apparatus. Scientists were also able to observe cell division and the splitting of chromosomes in both animal and plant cells. Through these observations, scientists gained a greater understanding of reproduction and inheritance and more pieces of Darwin's evolutionary theory fell into place.

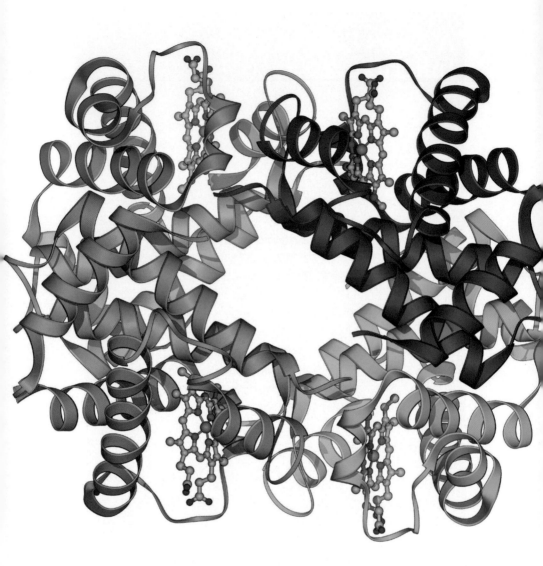

People with sickle-cell anemia have abnormal hemoglobin (pictured), which results in red blood cells shaped like stiff crescents.

(It's important to note that while the relationship between DNA and protein formation is important when talking about genetic inheritance of traits, not all DNA codes for proteins. Non-coding DNA perform other functions important to life, however, including gene regulatory sequences and production of noncoding RNA.)

Mutations naturally occur in our genetic material and arise from three types of events: errors during DNA replication, errors during reproduction, and through transposition (the movement of DNA elements within the genome). The mutations are embodied by changes in the DNA and, subsequently, RNA and the organism itself. Because mutations occur in the DNA, at the level of the genetic material, they are hereditary and the organism with the mutation can pass the same mutation on to its own offspring.

An example of a simple mutation with a powerful effect is the change of the base A to base T in the DNA coding strand for the β-globin protein. When this swap occurs, the mRNA created is different and therefore the amino acid sequence of the protein changes. Those who inherit this mutation in one allele are resistant to malaria, which is an advantage in areas where malaria is common. Those who inherit the mutation in both alleles have sickle-cell anemia, which causes many acute and chronic health problems and is a disadvantage. (This specific mutation is unusual for having both a positive and negative effect—most mutations are actually harmful.)

There are many other types of mutations, including insertions or deletions of a single base or many bases and rearrangements of DNA. Overall, however, the mutation rate in most organisms is low because the body has protective mechanisms that work to reduce and repair these changes as they happen. Nonetheless, mutations do occur, and they are the ultimate source of the variation that drives evolution.

Variation from Meiosis

In sexually reproducing populations, most of the genetic differences between individuals are from the reproductive process, not recent mutations. In sexual reproduction, parent organisms usually vary in many of their genes. Each parent organism has the opportunity to pass on some of its genes to offspring during reproduction, namely the process called meiosis. This is why one set of human parents might have one child with red hair and another with blonde hair, for example: each child received a different mix of genes from the same two parents.

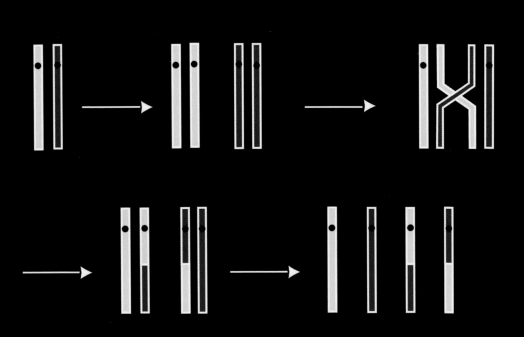

Barbara McClintock and Harriet Creighton were the first to show recombination occurring during meiosis in experiments on maize in 1931.

In meiosis, a parent cell undergoes two rounds of cell division to produce four daughter cells known as gametes. (Gametes are germ cells such as ova or sperm that can unite in a fertilization event to form a **zygote**, which in multicellular organisms is the first stage of organism development.)

Cells, as we recall, contain chromosomes, which in turn contain DNA. Before the cell divides, the DNA in the parent cell replicates to create two identical sister **chromatids** (copies of the replicated chromosome). In the first round of division, the newly replicated chromosomes pair up and swap segments of DNA in a process called **chromosomal crossover**. Next, they divide into two cells with the paired sister chromatids inside. The two cells divide again, and the sister chromatids separate to form four gamete cells. Each gamete cell now has half the number of chromosomes of the parent cell, randomly assorted through chromosomal crossover.

Meiosis increases genetic diversity and ensures that each gamete cell contains DNA from all four grandparents. (For, of course, the parent organism contains a mixture of DNA from both of its parents.) In doing so, it inserts a huge amount of variation into a population.

Honey Badgers: Uniting Darwinian Natural Selection and Mendelian Genetics

There are many examples of the interplay of genetics and natural selection. One interesting example of evolution in a genetic trait due to environment is in the honey badger's resistance to cobra venom. Honey badgers share a habitat with cobras, a type of venomous snake. When a cobra bites another animal, the neurotoxins it emits paralyze the diaphragm, preventing the animal from breathing. In the interest of survival, honey badgers, as well as hedgehogs and pigs, have evolved changes in specific amino acids that prevent the toxin from affecting their breathing. (All three animals evolved the change independently.)

The cause of the amino acid change is a mutation in the gene that helps form receptors where the neurotoxin usually binds and begins affecting the diaphragm. Due to the mutation, the form of the receptor changed and the neurotoxin can no longer take effect. The mutation appeared in the population and created a competitive advantage for the individuals who had it in their genome. Through natural selection, the proportion of honey badgers with the mutation grew until the mutation was a part of the general honey badger population.

In turn, the snakes have evolved more toxic venom, creating a bit of an evolutionary arms race.

EVOLUTIONARY SCIENCE EVOLVES OVER TIME

As we recall from the previous chapter, many scientists initially accepted Darwin's model of evolution, of the change of species over time, but most did not accept that natural selection was the true mechanism driving evolution.

Once scientists in the late nineteenth century and first half of the twentieth century better understood how cellular biology works, they were able to see that natural selection could act on genetic variation to increase the proportion of better adapted individuals in a population, and that over time, the accumulation of variations could create new species.

Since the time of Darwin and Mendel, scientists have added many discoveries to population genetics, cellular biology, and evolution.

They know that phenotype is a result of the interaction between genotype (its genetic code) and the environment. They've learned that each gene can have multiple alternate forms (alleles) and that there is not a 1:1 correlation between genes and traits. Some traits are affected by multiple genes, and some genes affect multiple traits. Most variations, in fact, are caused by multiple alleles with small effects, which makes it hard to link a specific allele with a specific phenotypic characteristic.

Scientists have also discovered that the genetic code is identical (or nearly so) across species. They've begun to question the importance of regulatory genes, which may be as important (or more so) in powering evolution than the genes that code for RNA. In the next chapter, we'll look at some of the new theories and discoveries and how they impact modern science and daily life.

Humans didn't evolve from apes, though both lineages share a common ancestor. Our ancestors instead include species like *Australopithecus afarensis*.

CHAPTER 5

Evolution's Influence Today

The major foundation-building discoveries in the theory of evolution fell into place between Darwin's publication of *On the Origin of Species* and the Modern Synthesis in the 1930s and 1940s. Since then, scientists have gained a better understanding of the age of the earth, learned more about how life began and evolved into complex forms, and found new evolutionary forces in addition to natural selection. They've also discovered important ramifications of evolution in health care, society, and our environment.

The ORIGINS of LIFE on EARTH

It is often said that all the conditions for the first production of a living organism are present, which could ever have been present. But if (and Oh! what a big if!) we could conceive in some warm little pond, with all sorts of ammonia and phosphoric salts, light, heat, electricity, etc., present, that a protein compound was chemically formed ready to undergo still more complex changes.

—*Charles Darwin in a letter to botanist Joseph Hooker*

Geologic Time Scale

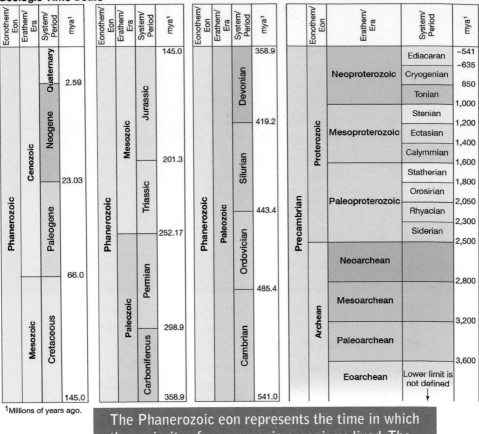

[1] Millions of years ago.

The Phanerozoic eon represents the time in which the majority of macroscopic organisms lived. The time before the Phanerozoic is the Precambrian.

The diversity of life readily apparent on earth today can make it seem impossible that all life on earth comes from a single common ancestor. And yet, when we look at dogs and wolves, we can see from their appearance how logical it is that they are related and share a common ancestor. The same is true for dogs and lizards, even humans and lizards, if we go back far enough in time.

Our understanding of the origins of life has become much more clear over the last century. As our understanding of the earth's ancient history and the formation of the universe grew, scientists have been able to put forth better hypotheses about life's origins. The dream Charles Darwin shared with Joseph Hooker of how the earth may have been created is not far from the theory held most commonly by modern science.

The earth itself is about 4.3 to 4.5 billion years old. Scientists believe that it was formed from meteorites and other material present in the early solar system coalescing under the force of gravity. As the earth formed, meteorites and other large objects pelted the young planet, and it was very hot and dry.

The earth's conditions became more amenable to life over the next billion years, and scientists estimate that life originated sometime between approximately 4 billion years ago (when the meteorological bombardment ended) and approximately 3.8 billion years ago (the formation of the earliest known fossils).

How did life begin? Given the right conditions, namely liquids, chemical elements, and energy, the resulting chemistry creates life.

In one famous experiment, Stanley Miller at the University of Chicago created an environment he thought modeled the early earth's conditions. He mixed methane, ammonia, and hydrogen gases with boiling water and used electricity to simulate lightning passing through the mixture. After a few days, the results included the formation of many different amino acids, including modern proteins. Miller's experiment (also known as the Miller-Urey experiment to credit the help of Miller's professor Harold Urey) changed the way scientists viewed the possible origins of life and showed that nonorganic materials could convert into the building blocks of life.

There is evidence of compositions similar to Miller's experimental conditions on both meteorites that have collided with earth and in deep-sea ocean vents. Of the two, deep-sea ocean vents are the more likely place for the origin of life. With the right conditions in place, the compounds formed and continued to evolve into a world with RNA and DNA (which we'll discuss in greater detail in a subsequent section) and protein-based life. This last stage is estimated to have occurred about 3.6 billion years ago, which was also the period of our last universal common ancestor.

From the last universal common ancestor begins a process of species evolution, divergence, and extinction. Scientists have found evidence of multicellular life dating as far back as 600 million years ago in China. Evidence of large organisms appears about 575 million years ago.

The geological time known as the Cambrian era, which began 542 million years ago, bore witness to an explosion of diversity of life. In this period, all the major body plans (groups of structural and developmental characteristics) appeared. Most living organisms during the Cambrian era lived in the sea, such as trilobites and crinoids. Toward the end of the Cambrian era, however, arthropods made it on to land. (Arthropods are invertebrate animals that include insects and arachnids.) Vertebrates made it onto land about 350 million years ago, and here the earth witnessed the evolution of fish into tetrapods (four-limbed vertebrates). Tetrapods diverged into different lineages that eventually evolved into mammals, lizards, birds, and more.

The process is much fuller and more complex than just described, and it is worth studying in greater detail. It serves to illustrate, however, how over a massive time scale, mutations and variations accumulated to create a stunning diversity of life forms.

CHANGING UNDERSTANDING of EVOLUTION

In the first half of the twentieth century, the understanding of evolution was roughly the combination of Darwin's theory of evolution via natural selection plus Mendelian genetics. Since that time, scientists have studied many other factors that impact the evolution of species. Some of the discoveries, such as tectonic plate movement and random **genetic drift**, are commonly accepted facts. Others, such as **neutral theory**, are still under debate in the scientific community.

Random Genetic Drift

Over time, populations change due to relatively random factors. For example, individuals reproduce at rates that have little to do with fitness. Think about your extended family. It's likely that some of your relatives have more children than others do, regardless of their age or health. The same is true in other species as well. This means that some genes will be passed on more than other genes without any correlation to health or beneficial advantages.

Additionally, in the case of sexual reproduction, each parent's alleles have only a 50 percent chance of being passed on to their offspring. This element of chance creates random changes in allele frequencies in a population, with some alleles disappearing and some becoming the only allele for that gene in the population. Statistically, an uncommon allele can more easily be lost by chance regardless of its benefits to the organism due to the chance factor in genetic inheritance.

The changes in a population that result from these random factors is called random genetic drift. Over time, random genetic drift can create a population that is genetically distinct from an original population.

Gene Flow

Gene flow is the movement of individuals or their genetic material from one population to another, which diffuses specific genes throughout greater geographic regions. Gene flow occurs whenever people (or their genes) migrate from one city to another, when animals enter a new territory, or when seeds of a plant blow in the wind to a new area.

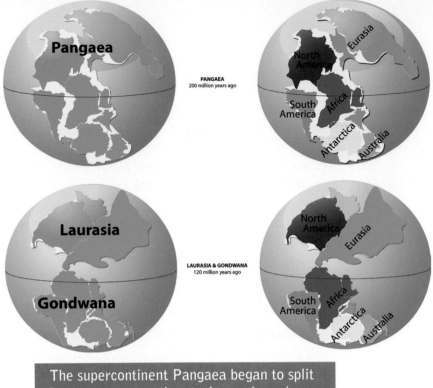

PANGAEA
200 million years ago

LAURASIA & GONDWANA
120 million years ago

The supercontinent Pangaea began to split into two megacontinents, Laurasia and Gondwana, in the Late Triassic period.

Plate Tectonics and Continental Drift

In 1912, Alfred Wegener proposed that the continents had at one time been one unified "supercontinent," Pangaea. Pangaea formed due to the collision of tectonic plates that, by the early Permian Era (299 to 252 million years ago), turned the separate continents into a unified landmass.

Wegener's theory was inspired by the similarity of the eastern coastline of South America and the western coastline of Africa, and the similarities between fossils in Brazil and West Africa. Continental movement, unification, and separation help explain how there are similar species on continents separated by oceans and why those species vary by location. Even though the species descended from common ancestors when the continents were together, the separation has created geographically isolated environments in which they have evolved independently.

Neutral Theory

Japanese biologist Motoo Kimura put forth what he called the neutral theory of molecular evolution, or neutral theory, in 1968.

According to Kimura, the majority of evolutionary mutations are caused by the random fixation (permanence within a population) of neutral or nearly neutral mutations. A neutral or nearly neutral mutation is one that has no advantage or disadvantage, and thus won't be acted on by natural selection.

Kimura's neutral theory selection argues that the most common nucleotide changes are changes in noncoding regions of DNA that have no effect on protein formation. These neutral mutations are fixed in a population or lost based on chance. Most changes disappear, and some remain. Over time, these neutral mutations accumulate and the genetic composition of a population changes dramatically over tens of millions of years.

Kimura's work uncovers new information about how the genetic composition of a population may be changing over great periods of time due to random mutations at the molecular level that have no advantageous effect on phenotype.

Neutral theory is linked to the discovery of a (metaphorical) **molecular clock** in the 1960s. The molecular clock shows that proteins change in their amino acid sequence at a constant rate over time. This is true even of a single protein that is evolving separately in distinct organisms. The molecular clock and mutation rate can be used to calculate the time at which two lineages diverged.

Punctuated Equilibrium

Darwin's theory of evolution emphasizes the effects of continuous, gradual change that accumulates within a population. Some argued that his theory could not be correct because there is evidence that species often remained unchanged for millions of years at a time and then changed rapidly into new forms. To describe this process, Niles Eldredge and Stephen Jay Gould proposed a theory they called **punctuated equilibrium**.

According to Eldredge and Gould:

> The history of life is more adequately represented by a picture of "punctuated equilibria" than by the notion of **phyletic gradualism** [a mode of evolution that relies on slow, gradual change in a species over time]. The history of evolution is not one of stately unfolding, but a story of homeostatic equilibria, disturbed only "rarely" (i.e., rather often in the fullness of time) by rapid and episodic events of speciation.

In his writing, Darwin dismissed the lack of evidence for transitional forms between different species as the result of an imperfect fossil record. Eldredge and Gould believed that a more likely explanation for a lack of transitional fossil forms was that new species were formed in a relatively abrupt segue from one form to another.

They proposed that new species emerge mainly when a population diverges from a parent species due to isolation at the edge of the parent population's geographic range. Most morphological changes happen very early on (and quickly) while the population is still small and adapting to its new conditions. Afterward, there is little gradual change in either the parent or diverged population. The rapid speed at which this mode of speciation happens makes it likely that no evidence will be found in the fossil record. The fossil record is not imperfect, then; it is telling of breaks in morphology due to rapid change.

Between periods of rapid change, they suggest that species stay relatively stable due to the ability of species and individuals to resist change through self-regulation. Factors that make this **homeostasis** (a state of equilibrium, or balance, in a population or group) likely include the effect of heterozygous genotypes (which keep variation present in the population) and natural selection's preference for intermediate phenotypes over extremes. Additionally, in most cases, there aren't enough new environmental pressures for natural selection to affect great change except in those isolated, peripheral geographic areas.

The Definition of a Species

The definition of what constitutes a species is an ongoing debate. One common approach, like Darwin's, is to define species as groups of organisms that resemble each other. This can be complicated, however, as it's hard to define how much organisms must resemble each other (or not) to be called one species or separate species. Another approach relies on modern technology to look at molecular divergence to see how similar species are in their DNA or RNA sequences. This too can be complicated, however, as there's not an easy threshold of genetic similarity that unites or divides groups into species.

The most commonly used way to define a species is via reproductive isolation. Ernst Mayr, a leading twentieth-century evolutionary biologist, wrote that a species is a group of organisms that interbreed in nature and are not reproductively able to interbreed with other such groups. This definition works only for organisms that reproduce sexually, and even in such organisms, it can still pose difficulties. There are many blurry lines between species, and hybridization between known species happens frequently.

Researchers are constantly learning about human evolution. Recent discoveries include the role of Neanderthal DNA in human immune responses.

HUMAN EVOLUTION

Human evolution is a fascinating topic in evolution as it focuses on perhaps our favorite species to study: ourselves. We have evolved from ancient, common ancestors, and there is an enormous fossil record to show it.

When Darwin wrote *On the Origin of Species* he avoided discussing human evolution. At the time, very few **hominin** fossils had been discovered or studied, so though a theory of human evolution was as logical as his theories around the evolution of other species, Darwin focused the book on species that had more significant observation-based evidence.

The evidence for human evolution soon appeared, however. The first hominin fossil, a skullcap, was discovered in 1856 (three years before Darwin published *On the Origin of Species)* in the Neander Valley in Germany. Its brow structure was notably different from human skulls, though it was clearly similar and related to humans. Darwin later wrote on human evolution in *The Descent of Man and Selection in Relation to Sex,* which he published in 1871. In this book, Darwin argued that humans evolved from a common ancestor that we shared with the apes, likely out of Africa. Today, with significantly more specimens in the fossil record, we see that he was right.

Humans belong to the Primate order, which also contains gorillas, chimpanzees, monkeys, lemurs, and more. About five to eight million years ago, a split in primate lineages created a fork with one lineage (the hominins) that eventually led to humans and another lineage that led to chimpanzees.

The taxonomy of which hominin species existed at different times in history has been and still is a topic of great scientific interest and debate. What follows here is a highly condensed overview of hominin evolution over millions of years. Though brief, the overview illustrates some key points around time spans, important traits, and the coexistence of hominin lineages.

Larger hominin brains and human-like body proportions appeared in *Homo erectus* (*second from right*) about 1.7 million years ago.

The first hominin fossil that scientists confidently declared a new species of human was discovered in 1925 by Raymond Dart. He found the remains of *Australopithecus africanus*, which he suggested was the link between apes and humans. It had a small brain and a prominent jaw and brow. Yet its teeth were similar to human teeth, and its skeletal structure suggested it was **bipedal** (it walked upright), a trait thought to define hominin lineages from other primates. Its brain, while small, looked more like a human brain than an ape brain.

A precursor to *A. africanus* was discovered in Ethiopia in 1974. The discovery of the fossil, known as "Lucy," was one of the most famous developments in human evolution. Lucy is a partial *Australopithecus afarensis* skeleton that dates back to about 3.3 million years ago. Her skeleton suggests that she was about three and a half feet tall, and the remains of her pelvis and lower limbs show she was bipedal, making *A. afarensis* one of the first known bipedal hominins. A set of preserved fossil footprints also show that *A. afarensis* walked and ran like modern humans. *A. afarensis* persisted in a relatively stable form for more than a million years before the lineage evolved and split.

The *Homo* lineage came much later and experienced significant evolution in both biology and culture over the last several million years. *Homo habilis* was the first species in the *Homo* genus. *H. habilis* existed roughly two million years ago and had a brain slightly larger than the *Australopithecus* species. It was one of the first hominin species to make tools, and they also butchered animals.

The *Homo* lineage continued to evolve with increased cognitive abilities and social organization. Several archaic *Homo* species, including *Homo erectus*, *Homo heidelbergensis*, and *Homo neanderthalensis*, lived in overlapping spans before the appearance of modern humans. *Homo erectus* eventually gave rise to *Homo sapiens*, our own species of modern humans.

The oldest known anatomically modern humans were found in Ethiopia and date back to about two hundred thousand years ago. They coexisted (and interbred) with the Neanderthals. Most of us have between 1 and 4 percent Neanderthal DNA in our genome.

Though we have remained the same species for the last two hundred thousand years, natural selection and other forces continue to shape human variation. One classic example of evolution is lactose intolerance, which affects most humans across the globe. Northern European populations are an exception—most people of northern European descent can digest lactose well into adulthood. This difference in lactose digestion correlates to variation in an allele of the LCT gene.

IMPLICATIONS of EVOLUTION on HEALTH CARE

Our understanding of evolution at a genetic level has provoked significant advancements in the health care industry. Evolution impacts areas of health care from how doctors diagnose and study diseases to the development of vaccines and medications to the treatment plans doctors prescribe.

Evolution of Diseases

All living things, including bacteria, evolve. One of the major health issues facing hospitals and communities today is antibiotic resistance, a natural property of some bacteria that has been accelerated by the pressures of natural selection.

Antibiotics, such as penicillin and amoxicillin, are important medications for treating infections. Doctors might prescribe antibiotics to treat streptococcal infections (strep throat) or before surgeries to prevent against infection, among other uses.

Bacteria can be resistant to certain antibiotics, however. Some bacteria naturally have this resistance, while others acquire it through genetic mutations or from another bacterium via a conjugation process that transfers genetic material between bacteria. Thus, bacteria can both pass on resistance to their offspring and transmit it to other living bacteria.

Those bacteria that are resistant to the specific antibiotic doctors prescribe to treat an infection survive and continue to multiply (and pass on their resistance) while the nonresistant bacteria die. Bacteria multiply quickly, and soon, the result is a population of antibiotic-resistant bacteria. Complicating matters, bacteria are often resistant to more than one antibiotic.

Antibiotic resistance has a significant impact on community health. The introduction of penicillin in the 1940s was heralded as one of the most important advances in medicine because it allowed doctors to treat infections and save more lives. However, if the bacteria growing in our communities are resistant to the drug we use to treat them, our doctors are unable to treat patients as effectively.

The Centers for Disease Control and Prevention (CDC) estimates that antibiotic-resistant bacteria cause at least twenty-three thousand deaths each year in the United States. If we focus on preventing infections and improving how doctors prescribe antibiotics, the CDC estimates that we could save thirty-seven thousand lives in the United States over five years.

Doctors today are encouraged to prescribe antibiotics in a careful, controlled manner and to be aware of antibiotic resistance patterns in their facilities and geographic regions to help ensure patients get the best drug and dosage to treat their infection.

Another type of disease evolution is exemplified by the Ebola virus. Ebola is a severe, life-threatening illness that has broken out several times in the last several decades. Each time a new outbreak occurs, it becomes a matter of great global concern because we don't have a vaccine to prevent Ebola or a good cure.

Ebola evolves, like other organisms, through mutations that arise during the RNA replication process (Ebola does not have DNA). The mutations provide genetic variation that natural selection and other evolution forces act on until mutations become highly prevalent in populations.

Ebola is evolving more quickly now than when it first emerged in 1976. One of the possible causes for its increased evolution rate is that Ebola is new to humans. Ebola used to be a disease found in wild animals, likely fruit bats, and the virus had adapted to its host environment. Once it was transmitted to humans and had a new environment with new conditions, it less fully adapted. Mutations had greater potential to affect survival, and Ebola began to evolve more quickly due to stronger selective pressures.

As Ebola evolves, the mutations in the disease could make it harder for medical professionals to identify the disease. The mutations also affect efforts to develop a vaccine and cure for Ebola.

Many other diseases evolve, as both viruses and bacteria are living organisms. Understanding their evolution helps medical professionals develop vaccines, cures, and treatment protocols to improve the health of humans across the globe.

DNA Testing

Studying evolution and understanding the genetic basis of mutations has also helped us understand how certain diseases arise in populations. Some diseases, called Mendelian diseases, are the result of a mutation in a single gene. When a child inherits two mutant copies of that gene, such as CFTR, which causes cystic fibrosis, he or she will have the disease.

Most diseases, however, are caused by the interplay of multiple alleles, each of which increases the risk for the disease when present. Identifying alleles that confer risk for a disease helps doctors to determine a treatment plan or estimate disease risk for their patients.

A common example in modern health care is the identification of mutations in the BRCA genes and the treatment decisions that follow. Women who have inherited mutations in the BRCA1 or BRCA2 genes have a greater risk of developing breast cancer and ovarian cancer than the general population. If a woman has a high risk of breast cancer based on personal or family history, she may be tested.

If the mutations in the BRCA1 or BRCA2 genes are present, doctors recommend certain treatment protocols to help prevent or detect the disease. Women who have mutations in the BRCA1 or BRCA2 genes may get increased screenings to help detect any cancer as early as possible, they might take certain medications to lower the risk of getting the cancer, or they might even undergo preventative surgery to reduce the risk of developing cancer even more.

The rising interest in knowing more about our DNA and genetics has birthed a new type of service: personalized genetic testing. The most common example at present is 23andMe, a company that collects saliva samples from its customers, conducts genetic testing, and sends back DNA-related results, such as whether the consumer is a carrier for a genetic condition like cystic fibrosis and whether or not he or she is lactose intolerant.

EVOLUTION and RACE

Evolutionary theories have often been used to justify classifications and unequal treatments of different races. For example, many polygenists (people who believed that human races evolved from different origins) supported slavery because they believed that other races were inferior and it was acceptable to treat them like animals. In fact, **polygenism** was especially popular in the United States because it supported the institution of slavery. Even some monogenists (people who believed that humans derived from a common origin) approved of slavery because they believed that within the human species, some races had degenerated and were better off ruled by masters. There were also, fortunately, supporters of **monogenism** and polygenism who believed that slavery was morally unjustifiable and worked to end the practice.

In the twentieth century, the eugenics movement surged. Eugenicists advocated for the improvement of the human race by promoting higher rates of reproduction in people with so-called desirable traits and preventing reproduction in those with so-called undesirable traits. The movement rendered terrible effects. During the Holocaust, the Nazi Party in Germany systematized eugenics in its efforts to kill all people who were not able-bodied, strong-minded members of the "Aryan" race. Eugenics was also common in immigration policies, such as those of the United States. Early in the twentieth century, the United States set up quotas that limited how many immigrants the United States would accept from countries whose citizens were considered to be of an inferior race.

Faced with this history, it's important to point out that race is not defined by a set of characteristics. Race is shaped by many factors, including biology, environment, and social conditions. When looking at how different skin colors evolve, many scientists focus on natural selection acting on populations. Other possible influential factors include sexual selection (selection based on preferences in one sex for certain traits in the other sex, such as the showy tail of the peacock). It is also possible that random differences in the small initial populations of humans played a role in creating skin color variation.

Stephen Jay Gould, one of the scientists who proposed punctuated equilibrium, said in an interview with PBS, "I think we have seen just how shallow and superficial the average differences are among human races, even though in certain features, like skin color and hair form, the visual differences are fairly striking. They're based on almost nothing in terms of overall genetic variation."

According to Gould:

> It looks as though all non-African diversity is a product of the second migration of *Homo sapiens* out of Africa—a migration so recent that there just hasn't been time for the development of much genetic variation except that which regulates some very superficial features like skin color and hair form. For once the old cliché is true: under the skin, we really are effectively the same. And we get fooled because some of the visual differences are quite noticeable.

It is now commonly accepted that modern humans evolved about two hundred thousand years ago in Africa and dispersed from Africa about one hundred thousand years ago. Any non-African diversity likely came from that dispersal one hundred thousand years ago, which isn't very much time from an evolutionary point of view. We are a single species, very much the same, with natural variation across and within populations.

The IMPLICATIONS of GLOBAL WARMING on EVOLUTION

If evolution is caused by changes in a population's environment, then it's a logical conclusion that the climate change underway on our planet has an impact on the species living on it.

Climate change brought on by methane gas and dust clouds has created extinction events earlier in the world's history. The modern era of climate change, driven largely by

Scientists believe polar bears diverged from brown bears forty-five thousand years ago due to changing climate patterns that made Arctic adaptations advantageous.

carbon emissions, is also taking an effect. Camille Parmesan, a professor in integrative biology at the University of Texas at Austin, writes:

> Ecological changes in the phenology and distribution of plants and animals are occurring in all well-studied marine, freshwater, and terrestrial groups. These observed changes are heavily biased in the directions predicted from global warming and have been linked to local or regional climate change through correlations between climate and biological variation, field and laboratory experiments, and physiological research.

The habitats of many organisms, especially those in polar and mountaintop environments, are disappearing as the earth warms. Some of the species living in these environments have gone extinct due to their shrinking habitats. Polar bears are a classic example of a species with a shrinking range. As ocean temperatures rise due to climate change, the Arctic sea ice continues to shrink, and polar bears are losing their primary platform for hunting. The effect is a significant reduction in polar bear population size and health.

Rising ocean temperatures and the increased frequency and severity of El Niño events have also caused extinction in much of the world's corals. It's estimated that 27 percent of the world's coral reefs are lost already, and another 30 percent are in danger of extinction in the next thirty years. Coral reefs provide food and habitat for many other species and protect coastlines from storms and erosion, and they have many other valuable roles to fish and humans.

The evidence of changing (and shrinking) habitats and extinctions is vast. Now, the question is whether our species will produce enough innovation and collaboration to reverse the climate change trajectory that we are on.

Creationist Opposition to Evolution

In the United States, the creationist movement is strongly opposed to how evolution is taught in schools. **Creationism**, or the belief that the world was created by God in the manner described in the Bible, first surged in the United States in the 1920s. The religious fervor culminated in the trial of John Scopes, a Tennessee science teacher who went on trial in 1925 for teaching evolution in a public school. The case was a major media sensation and a significant moment in the struggle between creationism and evolution. Scopes was convicted, but the attempt to quash teaching of evolution backfired. Public interest in Darwin and evolution surged again.

Creationism has waned and surged since that time. In more recent years, in 1999, the Kansas Board of Education voted to remove all mentions of evolution from school curriculum. The decision was reversed, but it highlights how the way evolution is taught remains contentious in American schools.

Creationists have continued to try to change the way science is taught by asking for equal treatment of intelligent design (creation by a sentient being) theories in academic textbooks. A federal district judge declared teaching intelligent design unconstitutional in 2005 because it violates that First Amendment's separation of church and state. Since then, other creationist efforts have included asking that the "strengths and weaknesses" of evolution be taught in schools, though evolution is widely accepted in the scientific community and its existence is not under debate.

CONCLUSION

> Whilst this planet has gone cycling on accordance to
> the fixed law of gravity, from so simple a beginning
> endless forms most beautiful and wonderful have
> been, and are being evolved.
> —*Charles Darwin*

Evolution has relevance to every form and every aspect of biological life, from the health of the environment to health care and more. One of the biggest questions of our time is how will human evolution proceed over the next centuries and millennia. In more economically developed countries, many of the traditional causes of natural selection, namely resource scarcity and predators, have been removed. Diseases continue to circle the globe, however, and it's possible that epidemics will affect the evolution of our immune systems.

Advancements in transportation technology have made geographic isolation, another factor in species divergence, harder to find. Sexual selection remains strong, however, and as technology becomes more complex and more ingrained in our culture, there may be greater pressures to choose mates based on intelligence and technological abilities.

Many look to technology itself as the next source of evolutionary change in humans, but as of yet, the technology we use is not a part of our hereditary genetic material. Technology does impact evolution today, however, both by creating new environmental conditions and by presenting greater information about our genome and how to control it. Scientists will continue to study how to modify the human genome to eliminate the diseases and disorders that lead to aging and death. It's possible that parents will be able to control increasingly more aspects of reproduction to control for desirable traits in their offspring.

And, of course, space travel is increasingly in the news as companies like SpaceX set their minds on making it possible for humans to live on other planets. When (assuming it will happen) that becomes reality, there could eventually become a scenario in which humans take one-way trips to start new colonies across the universe, creating a whole new level of geographic isolation.

Plant and animal life will continue to evolve as well, though there is perhaps less popular interest around these topics. As the environment continues to change, there will be new conditions to which organisms must adapt or face extinction. Evolution will also continue across species due to **genetic recombination**, gene flow, and other forces for change in the genome.

There is much speculation on how evolution will unfold over the next centuries, millennia, and millions of years. Though we can only make educated hypotheses as to how life on earth will change over that time, one thing is certain: evolution will continue and the world will change.

Chronology

4.5 billion years ago	Earth forms
3.8 billion years ago	Life forms and begins to diversify
8 to 6 million years ago	Last common ancestor of humans and chimpanzee
200,000 years ago	Modern humans, *Homo sapiens*, appear
100,000 years ago	Modern humans move out of Africa

150 BCE Ptolemy publishes *Almagest*, which lays out his geocentric theory of the structure of the universe

1543 Nicolaus Copernicus publishes *On the Revolutions of the Heavenly Spheres* with his heliocentric theory of the solar system and sparks the Copernican Revolution

1613 Galileo Galilei publishes *Letters on Sunspots*, which suggests the sun is not eternally, perfectly formed

1650s Archbishop James Ussher publishes chronologies declaring the creation of universe happened in 4004 BCE

1665 Robert Hooke publishes *Micrographia*, which details his observation of cork cells under a microscope

1687 Sir Isaac Newton publishes *Mathematical Principles of Natural Philosophy*

1735 Carl Linnaeus publishes his taxonomy in the *Systema Naturae*

1760 The Industrial Revolution begins

1801 Jean-Baptiste Lamarck publishes *Theory of Inheritance of Acquired Characteristics*

1809 Charles Darwin born in Shrewsbury, England

1822 Gregor Mendel born in Heinzendorf bei Odrau (today Hynčice, Czech Republic)

1830 Charles Lyell publishes *Principles of Geology*, a seminal text in geology

1831 Darwin sets off as a naturalist on the HMS *Beagle* on a five-year voyage to South America

1844 Robert Chambers publishes *Vestiges of the Natural History of Creation*

1856 First hominin fossil discovered in the Neander Valley

1859 Darwin publishes *On the Origin of Species*

1866 Mendel publishes *Experiments on Plant Hybridization*

1878 Ernst Karl Abbe invents the 100x oil immersion lens

1882 Darwin dies in London

1884 Mendel dies in Brno

1900 Several European scientists independently rediscover Mendel's work on plant genetics; William Bateson founds the discipline of genetics

1912 Alfred Wegener proposes that the continents had at one time been one unified "supercontinent," Pangaea

1925 Raymond Dart discovers the first *Australopithecus africanus*; John Scopes goes on trial for teaching evolution in a Tennessee public school

1930s to 1940s Modern Synthesis unites disciplines of lab-based and field-based evolutionary biology

1968 Motoo Kimura proposes his theory that most evolutionary change is due to neutral mutations

1972 Niles Eldredge and Stephen Jay Gould propose their theory of punctuated equilibrium

1999 The Kansas Board of Education votes to remove all mentions of evolution from school curriculum (the decision is reversed)

2006 23andme is founded to provide genetic testing and interpretation to consumers

Glossary

allele One of two or more possible versions of a gene. For example, humans have three basic alleles for blood type: A, B, and O.

bipedal A descriptor for animals that walk on only two legs.

blended inheritance An old and inaccurate theory that the characteristics of parents are blended in offspring. Blended inheritance was used to argue against Darwin's theory of natural selection.

catastrophism The theory that changes to the earth's surface over time resulted from sudden, catastrophic events such as massive floods.

chromatid One of two strands that results when a chromosome divides lengthwise during cell division, with each strand containing a DNA double helix.

chromosomal crossover The exchange of genetic material between homologous (corresponding) chromosomes that occurs during sexual reproduction.

Copernican Revolution The major shift in worldview sparked by Nicolaus Copernicus when he proposed that the sun, not the earth, was the center of the solar system.

creationism The belief that the universe and life began through the actions of a divine creator, such as depicted in the Bible.

DNA Deoxyribonucleic acid, the hereditary material usually found in the nucleus of cells. DNA carries the instructions for how organisms form, grow, and reproduce.

gene A specific segment of DNA; the basic unit of heredity that determines how proteins are formed.

gene flow The transfer of alleles or genes from one population to another due to migration.

genetic drift Variation in the frequency of different genotypes present in a population due to how often some individuals reproduce and pass on their genes compared to others in the population.

genetic recombination The process through which alleles are exchanged between two different chromosomes or (less frequently) between two regions of the same chromosomes.

genome The complete set of DNA (and genes) in an organism that contains all the information needed for the organism to form, grow, and reproduce.

genotype The genetic makeup of an organism, unseen by the naked eye.

geocentric A model of the universe with the earth at the center (incorrect but commonly accepted until the Copernican Revolution).

heliocentric A model of the universe with the sun at the center of the solar system.

heterozygous Having two different alleles of a gene at a given location.

homeostasis A state of equilibrium, or balance, in a population or group.

hominin The tribe made up of modern humans and our immediate ancestors, including the genera *Homo* and *Australopithecus*.

homozygous Having two of the same alleles of a gene at a given location.

meiosis A type of cell division in which one cell produces four cells with half the number of chromosomes as the parent cell.

molecular clock The rate at which a species' genome accumulates changes in protein sequences. The molecular clock can be used to calculate moments of divergence between species.

monogenism The belief that all races of humans descended from a common origin. Charles Darwin was a monogenist.

morphology The form or structure of a plant or animal; the study of the form and structure of plants and animals.

mutation An inheritable change in a single DNA base or a string of DNA. Mutations are a major source of variation in organisms and can be positive, negative, or neutral.

natural selection The process in which organisms that are more adapted to their environment survive to produce more offspring than their less adapted peers. Their offspring inherit the same advantages, which changes the makeup of the population of organisms over time.

neutral theory A theory of molecular evolution that argues that most evolutionary changes are caused by neutral or nearly natural mutations.

particulate inheritance The inheritance of traits through discrete genes that pass from one generation to the next without blending.

phenotype The observable characteristics of an organism that result from the interaction of their genotype and their environment.

phyletic gradualism A mode of evolution that relies on slow, gradual change in a species over time, usually involving the entire species.

polygenism The (inaccurate) belief that different races of humans evolved separately from different origins.

proletariat Working-class people.

punctuated equilibrium The hypothesis that evolution happens in bursts of rapid change between long periods of little evolutionary change.

saltationism A big change in a species that occurs in a compressed time frame.

taxonomy A system for classifying things, especially organisms, based on their relationships.

uniformitarianism The theory that changes to the earth's surface over time resulted from gradual, continuous processes that have always been acting on the earth.

vestigial The smallest trace of something that previously existed, such as an organ or body part; for example, the tiny leg bones near the tail end of snakes that show evidence that snakes descended from lizards and over time evolved to have (almost) no leg bones.

zygote A cell such as a fertilized ovum that results from the fusion of two gametes.

Further Information

BOOKS

deGrasse Tyson, Neil, and Donald Goldsmith. *Origins.*
Fourteen Billion Years of Cosmic Evolution. New York, NY:
W.W. Norton & Co., 2004.

Futuyma, Douglas J. *Science on Trial.* Sunderland, MA: Sinauer
Associates, Inc, 1995.

Nye, Bill. *Undeniable: Evolution and the Science of Creation.*
New York, NY: St. Martin's Press, 2014.

WEBSITES

Evolution Lab
www.pbs.org/wgbh/nova/labs/lab/evolution/

Play a game to learn the evolutionary relationships
between species.

Experts Tackle Question of How Humans Will Evolve
www.scientificamerican.com/article/predictions-experts-
tackle-question-of-how-humans-will-evolve/?WT.mc_id=SA_
printmag_2014-09

Browse an assortment of expert hypotheses for the future of
human evolution.

50 Years Ago: A Witness at the Scopes Trial
http://www.scientificamerican.com/article/50-years-ago-scope-trial-witness/

Hear about the prosecution of John Scopes for teaching evolution in a Tennessee public school from one of the trial's expert witnesses, American anthropologist Fay-Cooper Cole. Cole provides an entertaining narrative of how the trial unfolded and the effects it had on the American public.

VIDEOS

Evolution—What Darwin Never Knew
www.youtube.com/watch?v=AYBRbCLI4zU

The History of Our World in 18 Minutes
www.ted.com/talks/david_christian_big_history?language=en

Bibliography

Barton, Nicholas H., Derek E. G. Briggs, Jonathan A. Eisen, David B. Goldsetin, and Nipam H. Patel. *Evolution.* Cold Spring Harbor, NY: Cold Spring Harbor Laboratory Press, 2007.

Bowler, Peter J. *Evolution.* Berkeley, CA: University of California Press, 2003.

Braterman, Paul S. "How Science Figured Out the Age of Earth." *Scientific American*, October 20, 2013. Retrieved January 5, 2016 (http://www.scientificamerican.com/article/how-science-figured-out-the-age-of-the earth/).

Burkhardt, Jr., Richard W. Foreword to *Zoological Philosophy* by J.B. Lamarck, xv-xxxvii. Chicago, IL: University of Chicago Press, 1984.

Cesar, Herman, Lauretta Burke, and Lida Pet-Soede. "The Economics of Worldwide Coral Reef Degradation." Arnhem, The Netherlands: Cesar Environmental Economics Consulting, 2003. Retrieved January 5, 2016 (http://coralreef.noaa.gov/redirect.html?newURL=http://assets.panda.org/downloads/cesardegradationreport100203.pdf).

Chambers, Robert. *Vestiges of the Natural History of Creation.* London, England: John Churchill, 1844. Retrieved January 5, 2016 (https://archive.org/stream/ vestigesofnatura00unse/vestigesofnatura00unse_djvu.txt).

Darwin, Charles. *The Origin of Species and the Voyage of the Beagle.* New York, NY: Alfred A Knopf, 2003.

Darwin, Charles, and Francis Darwin. *Charles Darwin: Autobiography and Letters.* New York, NY: D. Appleton and Co., 1892.

Drabeck, Danielle H., Antony M. Dean, and Sharon A. Jansa. "Why the Honey Badger Don't Care: Convergent Evolution of Venom-Targeted Nicotinic Acetylcholine Receptors in Mammals that Survive Venomous Snake Bites." *Toxicon* 99 (2015): 68–72.

Eldredge, Niles, and Stephen Jay Gould. "Punctuated Equilibria: An Alternative to Phyletic Gradualism." In *Models in Paleobiology,* edited by Thomas J. M. Schopf, 82–115. San Francisco, CA: Freeman Cooper, 1972.

Hlodan, Oksana. "Evolution: Applications in Human Health and Populations." *Bioscience* 58 (2008): 480–483. Retrieved January 5, 2016 (doi: 10.1641/B580603).

Institute of Human Origins. "Lucy's Story." Retrieved January 5, 2016 (https://iho.asu.edu/about/lucys-story).

Jacobs, Kenneth H. "Human Origins." In *What Darwin Began,* edited by Laurie Rohde Godfrey, 274–292. Newton, MA: Allyn and Bacon, Inc., 1985.

James, Patricia. *Population Malthus.* London, England: *Routledge* & Kegan Paul, 1979.

Kennedy, Kenneth A. R. "The Dawn of Evolutionary Theory." In *What Darwin Began,* edited by Laurie Rohde Godfrey, 3–23. Newton, MA: Allyn and Bacon, Inc., 1985.

Kimura, Motoo. "Natural Selection and Neutral Evolution." In *What Darwin Began,* edited by Laurie Rohde Godfrey, 73–93. Newton, MA: Allyn and Bacon, Inc., 1985.

Lamarck, J. B. *Zoological Philosophy.* Translated by Hugh Elliot. Chicago, IL: University of Chicago Press, 1984.

Lyell, Charles. "Uniformity of Change." In *Scientific Papers* 38. New York, NY: P.F. Collier & Son, 1909. 14. Retrieved January 5, 2016 (http://www.bartleby.com/38/8/).

Malthus, T. R. *An Essay on the Principle of Population.* Oxford, England: Oxford University Press, 1993.

Mendel, Gregor. *Experiments in Plant Hybridization.* Translated by the Royal Horticultural Society. Cambridge, MA: Harvard University Press, 1926.

Orel, Vítězslav. *Gregor Mendel.* Translated by Stephen Finn. Oxford, England: Oxford University Press, 1996.

Owen, James. "Future Humans: Four Ways We May, or May Not, Evolve." National Geographic News, November 24, 2009. Retrieved January 5, 2016 (http://news. nationalgeographic.com/news/2009/11/091124-origin-of-species-150-darwin-human-evolution.html).

Parmesan, Camille. "Ecological and Evolutionary Responses to Recent Climate Change." *Annual Review of Ecology, Evolution and Systematics* 37 (2006): 637–69. Retrieved January 5, 2016 (doi: 10.1146/annurev. ecolsys.37.091305.110100).

PBS. "Interview with Stephen Jay Gould." Retrieved January 5, 2016 (http://www.pbs.org/race/000_About/002_04-background-01-09.htm).

Priscu, John C. "Origin and Evolution of Life on a Frozen Earth." National Science Foundation. Retrieved January 5, 2016 (http://www.nsf.gov/news/special_reports/darwin/textonly/polar_essay1.jsp).

Secord, James A. *Victorian Sensation.* Chicago, IL: University of Chicago Press, 2000.

Stamos, David N. *Evolution and the Big Questions.* Malden, MA: Blackwell Publishing, 2008.

peppered moth studies, 60, **60**

Phanerozoic eon, **86**

phenotype, 73, 82, 91, 93

phyletic gradualism, 92

plant genetics, 58–59, 71–73

plate tectonics, 88, 90

Plato, 10–11

polar bears, **103**, 104

polygenism, 100–101

population genetics, 60–61, 82

proletariat, 23

Ptolemy, 10–13, 15, 17

punctuated equilibrium, 91–93, 101

racism in theories of evolution, 42, 100–102

radiocarbon dating, **26**, 28

Ray, John, 30

reproduction process, debate about, 32–35

resources, competition for, 42, 44–45, 53, 65, 106

RNA, 79, 83, 87, 93, 99

saltationism, 54

scientific method, 6, 24, 55

Scientific Revolution, 5, 9–10, 14–23, 24, 27–28, 40, 49

Scopes, John, 105

sickle-cell anemia, **78**, 79

species, 34, 93

Darwin's definition of, 68–69, 93

how they change, 27–45

spontaneous generation, 34–35

taxonomy, 19–21, 30, 32, 95

"theory of form," 10–11

tortoises, giant, 50, 66, **67**

Tschermak, Erich von, 59

uniformitarianism, 21–22, 28 29

Ussher, James, 13–14, 21, 28

variation in populations, 7, 52–54, 56, 58–61, 63–66, 70–71, 73–79, 80–83, 88

Vestiges of the Natural History of Creation, 40–41, 53

vestigial, 70

Voyage of the Beagle, The, 52

Wallace, Alfred Russell, 53–54

Watson, James, 74

Wegener, Alfred, 90

Wright, Sewall, 60

zygote, 81

About the Author

Rachel Keranen is a writer based in Madison, Wisconsin. Her work focuses on science, software, and entrepreneurship. She's passionate about learning and loves taking deep dives into science and history, which made evolution a perfect fit for her interests. In addition to the books that she writes, Keranen's previous work includes articles in the *Minneapolis/St. Paul Business Journal* and the *London Business Matters* magazine.

Keranen enjoys traveling, being outdoors, and reading the *New York Times*. Her DNA test results show that she is 2.9 percent Neanderthal.